Cuban Journal

A POET IN THE

VENCEREMOS BRIGADE

1970

JOEL SLOMAN

Cuban Journal

A POET IN THE

VENCEREMOS BRIGADE

1970

ZOLAND BOOKS
Cambridge, Massachusetts

First edition published in 2000 by
Zoland Books, Inc.
384 Huron Avenue
Cambridge, Massachusetts 02138

The quotation on page 9 and repeated in part on page 26 is from
John Ashbery's poem "Evening in the Country," originally
published in *The Double Dream of Spring* (Dutton, 1970)

The poem about Mount Fuji on page 9 and the prose quotation
on page 17 are both from Nobuyuki Yuasa's translation of
Bashō's works, *The Narrow Road to the Deep North
and Other Travel Sketches* (Penguin, 1966).

FIRST EDITION

Book design by Boskydell Studio
Printed in the United States of America

07 06 05 04 03 02 01 00   8 7 6 5 4 3 2 1

This book is printed on acid-free paper, and its binding materials
have been chosen for strength and durability.

Library of Congress Cataloging-in-Publication Data

Sloman, Joel.
Cuban journal : a poet in the Venceremos Brigade, 1970 / Joel
Sloman — 1st ed.
p. cm.
ISBN 1-58195-015-2
1. Americans — Travel — Cuba — Poetry.   2. Venceremos
Brigade — Poetry.   3. Cuba — Poetry. I. Title.
PS3569.L64 C83 2000
811'.54 — dc21   99-089813

Thine

In 1969 and 1970, hundreds of Americans joined the Venceremos Brigade and traveled to Cuba to support its effort to harvest a record ten million tons of sugar cane. Their support was as direct as it could be. They worked in the cane fields beside Cubans and volunteers from other countries. I was one of many *brigadistas* to record their experiences. My journal was initially intended to be shared only with other members of the brigade. But no experience is so special it can't give pleasure and meaning to a wider audience.

This is essentially the text of the journal as it was written thirty years ago. Very few changes have been made, most of them technical; for example, I corrected the spelling of Spanish words and tried to treat titles or quotations more consistently. Only a handful of lines were actually revised, but only to clarify, not change, their meaning. When I was in Cuba I also kept a conventional prose diary. A few excerpts from this are inserted.

Carol's face went through one transformation after another. All of her history was there simultaneously. She was her own ancestor, babushka and all, and then she was Carol again, only very young and innocent.

I remember thinking about my father too. I believed that I understood him better than ever before.

In the middle of the night we walked down two twisting flights of stairs to the kitchen to get something to drink, then back up two flights of stairs to the attic. When the incredibly laborious trip was over, I had a sudden illumination — the meaning of civilization was "bringing water to the table."

The next day I thought I'd be "recognized" on the street because I was so shaky and paranoid. I seemed to exist inside a "sound envelope." My whole digestive system was spooked.

Carol went home to New York. "How could I be so stupid and reckless?" I asked myself in self-flagellating panic. Michele, who had dropped acid before, reassured me. My state of mind gradually improved throughout the day. Shamed by my poor judgment — a shock to my complacency — I went to sleep early to be ready for the next day's journey.

In the middle of the following afternoon, I was one of about 350 people in eleven buses that left Cambridge from Vassar St. near MIT for Saint John, New Brunswick. The press was there. The FBI was there too, and they followed us to the Canadian border. We picked up a lawyer in Bangor just in case.

Some people on our bus were suspicious of Elizabeth because she complained loudly and nonstop without the shadow of an inhibition. She was also older than most of us. I was nervous because I knew only a few people — members of my affinity group — but I didn't know them very well. I was a little bit on the old side too — twenty-six. Our average age was closer to twenty.

The trip went smoothly. Customs officers were polite. We got to Saint John at seven in the morning, but sat in our buses for several more hours until the returning first brigade got off our ship, the *Luis Arcos Bergnes*.

Then we were allowed to mingle with the veteran *brigadistas*, among whom were my friends Jerry and George. They seemed happy and healthy to me as they tried to figure out how to get their film safely back into the States. Members of both brigades exchanged information. What was cutting cane like? What was happening in Boston?

By the time we finally boarded, at about 9:00 PM, we felt more at ease. Our passports were checked. Then we got bunk assignments and explored the large dormitory below deck. It was like a locker room. There was no hot water.

In the dining room above, women ate first, men next — the gulls waited and screamed impatiently. There were continuous discussions, a couple of which I listened in on eagerly, curiously, critically. Then I climbed into my upper bunk and went to sleep. It was Thursday, February 12, 1970.

LUIS ARCOS BERGNES

February 13, 1970, at sea late at night

"They just don't realize the world's
gonna win!"
This in discussion
Venceremos Brigade ship
Luis Arcos Bergnes
A paper bag falls silently
down metal staircase
Cuban Latin music and dancing
Cubans Americans
long yellow hair
long black hair
short dark hair
dark skin
ashtrays
Havana cigars
and wine
a row of backs
and talking
small flute
"On the beach
I want to dance"
green canvas dripping
first day out
from Saint John New Brunswick
joy but no seasickness
no wine-sickness
no cigar-inhalation
moral dilemma
revolutionary discussion
women can cut cane too

"a cortar la caña va"
la Brigada Venceremos
Granada
Dark cave café of boat
green dining room
I like the people a lot
they like me too
the one from Pennsylvania
and those from Boston
or Cuba
"20 cigarros"
Aromas Rubios
buttons
stares
into the smoke-filled
combo area
blue coat old sailor
What does he do in Cuba?
wool
applause
violet posters collages
glasses
red hair
looking at me occasionally
"History Will Absolve Me"
in a puff of smoke
my father's scarf around my
unshaven neck
friends scrubbing tables
tentative communication
old '50s rock
sung in dormitories
Weathermen
earrings
painted screen for film

February 14, at sea in the morning

Cold up here
icy outside
except leaning on the kitchen wall
for steam heat
shoes cold on deck
lean lean lean
lean weather
gulls behind us
scavenging
waves heavy on one side
going away on the other
dark blue with fine foam patterns
going 12 miles out to horizon
I'm facing forward
in the dining room
rolling side to side
people standing reading Fidel's speeches
on the *Diez Millones*
or the tenth anniversary of the Revolution
Her checkers partner seasick
end of game
a new partner arrives
the old one comes back
the motor continues
man smoking mild or hard
cigarros
from Cuba
in package without cancer warning
Cancer may be in the sky tonight
over sea
stable in this rolling
"Hey! this really rockin in here!"

I don't know
I may get sick

but I hope not
the cold worrying me more and more
a scarf around my neck
two shirts and a sweater
my beard coming along
can't shave in such icy water
this is still the morning
I'll go out after lunch again
and whenever I feel sickness danger
in my head or stomach
no music yet today
in this metal craft
the poor cows suffered on too
even a seasick sailor
"Is there a Third World meeting this morning?"
the sea is even bigger than the revolution
and we can still kill it
in our showy Mexican blankets
not so far from our bad impulses
faces of anxiety
running stopping starting
down the aisles
laughter in the face of gales
that may show up here
checkers chess
slapping feet and hands for warmth
the sea
it's so impressive
we're not conquering it
we're coexisting
fragile floating seedling
on bear muscle and matted fur

February 15

Beige
my own portrait
covering anonymous gestures
very tight shoulders
I sit across
as always writing
"not relating"
a watch and Speidel watchband
the sea darkening
60 miles from shore
remembering lines and phrases out on deck

"I am still completely happy.
        . . .
Have you begun to be in the context you feel
Now that the danger has been removed?"

"In a way
It was nice
Not to see Mt. Fuji
In foggy rain"

All the people I like here
        with lips they tighten
    assured California voice
            LA voice
                Seattle voice
        smart Cambridge voice
            indifferent New York voice
            tough Chicago voice
                    I'm so safe
    how can we "trash" anything
            responding to Conspiracy verdict
                    on Cuban boat?
    Just each other
        what we hate in ourselves

How can we do that?
leaning over deck rail today
looking up from Bashō poem
seeing one, two, three
interesting people pass by
a Cuban brigade woman
with bleached hair
woman with straight hair from Seattle
straggly short-haired big blonde
with amazing expressive
joyous face
from Boston area
I felt I could just continue to watch
and the parade of interesting people
would go on and on
and I waited
but what was left was the thought
turning in on itself
Is my role to befriend
the type of personal fear confronting me now
reading Gus Hall on revolution?

February 16, 6 PM

Charlie Chaplin film
front of ship's dining room
cool in here now
day of mild squalls
now film over
people flowing to rear
outside to deck and dark sea
or tables to talk or read
or write journals
me in Brigade 6
I found out today

all from Boston
which means no Third World people
3 dolphins flashed rose/brown
briefly through
dark racing waves
going in our direction
waves dolphins seagulls
heading toward Florida coast
to veer away from and around it
to Cuba

*

Fearless azure
"Everybody's got a different style"
Spanish
superficial inborn manners
picking scabs on skin
for sore throat two different pills
and a red coating
swabbed on throat back
two, three times a day
plus tetanus injection
David peeling rusty potatoes
for our food
his "opportunist" brigade
broken up
in official arrangement
Weatherman beaten in argument
by Third World
now with meeting on kitchen roof
out on deck
blank look at the sea
placed in my head all day
shower after lunch
temperature mildness

and then a chill
changeable single fabric
with different reading material
strewn through young minds
Cuban artist reading
For Whom the Bell Tolls
in Cuban edition
I lose lunchtime hunger
only pure rice
arroz
appealing
later some tea and plain sea biscuits
longing for ITT Hostess cupcake
Schrafft's danish
even milk
from a cow
any nationality
the warm bland sweet starchy
revolutionary diet
salty strings of meat
now big dinner time line winds around room
"I didn't realize that!"
"This is something I never miss!"
Food!
I'm so unhungry
but I'll eat anyway
What is it?

February 17, mid-afternoon

The days fade into each other
not sleeping one night
makes a 48-hour day
with a blue handkerchief on her head
as always

                    talk as always
            winding on
                        like Mexican towns in the '30s or '40s
    in Hollywood novels
                full of expatriates
                        and nincompoops
                    drinking gambling whoring
            wasting away
                            poets revolutionaries
        I got the boat blues
            somewhere off Florida
            reading *Structural Anthropology*
                    and thinking
                            Tarot
                potatoes
                    dolphins
                            nautical miles
            books to edit
            for brigade record
                    good news
                            fists in the air
                    off the stern
                            crying gulls
                        dive for crackers
                        and swill
        the music without the country of origin
                under my feet
            a little crazy
                    like Spanish lessons
                        on deck last night
            Trude got sick
        with paranoid side effects
                        sweet processed fruit
            by side of metal food tray
    "Oye!
            campañeros"

Witness for the Prosecution
hissing cops
naiveté
left-wing cynicism of Billy Wilder
blank meditation wall
on meditation ocean
running to the edge
ooing over the brown dolphins
diving under boat
this is pure description
since my head's not completely together yet
though getting there
still special people I'd like to meet
and talk with
brown with pink scarf
tall youthful adolescent
pouting lips dark somber eyes
all people full of poetry
operatic histrionics blue hair and skin
wash brush soft short light locks
on big body about to jump
with it
onto stage
frizzled nightmares
of stench dormitories
using too much bourgeois cleansing water
no tub?
penny wise pound foolish
"Damn you!"
Marlene Dietrich
into Charles Laughton's face
Why did Cubans choose this film?
now people standing around
expecting life from me
and help and all sorts
of reinforcement

big shit
women using men's bathroom
we are all so liberated
and young
and smart
and hidden
without help
without self-discipline
in a radical body experiment
that primitive mask
of rhetoric
to bring it together
mask of theatrical gesture
shades mask
for our blank eyes
with acid I learn I can be a teacher
loving the child in people
more than the socialized layers
of fear and anxiety
(this is coming apart
under the stare
above around through
of brown tedious eyes
leaning on the wall
to my right
Attention!)

Feburary 18, a little after lunch

Feet waving from uppermost deck
distant stern of ship
just past Florida coast
head sinking in exercise thrill
of muscle
motion after sick throat

                                    sick breath
                        sick stomach
                              sick head politics
            and gradual paranoia disease
        foam white
                    on heaven-blue ocean
            calm as skin of pea
                              fresh from cosmic pod
    oil rig
                gay red and white
                in the gulf
                        songs shouts
                    from The Band
                              or Dylan
                    or '50s rock
    "*Ven-cer-e-mos!*"
                        with fists plugging atmosphere
                              to small
                    confused Florida fishing boats
    "Don't do that!"
                        Cubans say
                        political provocation
                                        etc.
        We love Miami too
                in our hearts
        beneath our filling station shirts
                              and engraved fist buttons
                    If I'm called to work
                        can I hear from here?
            under the blisters of someone's feet
        We've crossed a certain space
                              on the ocean
                        tuning in our radios to shore AM-FM
                    for Conspiracy news
                              and rock sounds
    But that space is like a void

                    devoid of history
              no civilization lived here
                        O Atlantis!
                 lost in its heaven-depths
                    mythology-shores
                                  the smell is divine and fresh
          I want to write a whole book about it
                    stale samples
                             sitting on bookshelves
                  small fishing boats
                      yachts
                              contending
                     to wave to us
            and getting back shocking chants
        a lonely gull
                        cigarette butt
                  purple bells
                          beards sticky hair
                                  smelly sweaters
                what seem like
                          mown Miami lawn shreds
                     floating in schools
                               or is it seaweed?
            small jerky push or bounce
                   of motor and sea screw
        "I didn't know where I was for five days!"
                 on bow slapping forehead
                      then she sings
                   does exercises
           I'm moving in strange ways
                           like God
                    Poseidon

". . . all who have achieved real excellence in any art possess
one thing in common, that is, a mind to obey nature, to be
one with nature, throughout the four seasons of the year."
                                            — Bashō

Overwhelming environment
I cough up some phlegm
and inspire
on leaving US coast
wanting to lie like a bubble of foam
on calm waters like these
heavy dormant hawser
white fishing boat splotch
I met another poet today at lunch
while some brigades work
at potato-cutting
washing sanding painting
for Havana arrival

*

6:30 this morning
old communist Farmers' Union brigade member
shouts through men's dormitory
"Get up!
Miami's out there!"
some mocking of Cuban call
"de pie!"
and many believe it's breakfast
go up and out on deck
to view green trees
mist above sandy beaches
and large white hotels and condominiums
under pollution cloud
we stare and grit teeth
tune in Miami news stations
and hear Conspiracy jury out
5th day
Kunstler asks mistrial
He may be debarred!
Humid morning

after guava juice
fish croquet
and sweet warm coffee-flavored drink to sip
I try to read in dining room
then a film false alarm
later through newly opened route
straight to cluttered bow
with masts up and folded
hawsers
cables
railings
anchor holes
hatches
green floors
gray vaults
rusty steel framework
and crowds of *brigadistas*
lolling
bobbing
staring
sunning themselves
confusion of US coast
sub-tropic breeze
oil façade
life in the sea
some spotted brown dolphins
faces full of shock
"We're here!"
this weather means vacation
brown burnt soup passes by
with green lettuce
over smoky deep turquoise sea
tiny crawling insect on my arm
being diffused to distant habitation
rose cloud on horizon
Lunch

after many a Miami song
rock or folk ode
to land we hate and/or love
We leave a wake!
We exist!
Luis Arcos Bergnes
cattle boat for the revolution
which will be one again
fifteen days after we leave it
brigade by brigade
tomorrow morning
greeted by joyous Cuban faces
whoops!
rushed onto buses
off to camp
Now meat/soup swill smell
tossed from pail
three gulls land in that watery spot
scrabbling for our garbage
I'm clearing my throat
from epidemic post-nasal drip
must see doctor again
a very serious but kindly person
with sacramental cough syrup offering
white double aspirin tablet
mysterious brown and pink pills
red antiseptic paint for back of gagging throat
"Mañana. OK?"
soft bells
a match struck
and smoke odor
sea
engine
marble foam over ripples
sailor whistles
into deck's curved distance

                              voice
                           cigar
                   man stroking beard
        long-light-brown-haired woman
                                   suspensefully holding book
                                          sitting by railing
                 as if awaiting voice from sea
                     By itself
                                 rope bends slightly
                      from breeze or boat listing
            scrunched mild Cuban *cigarros* package
                              lies hidden in nearby gutter
         light chain with cylindrical wooden plug
                     moves a little with ship
                                 another block is leaning
                                     motionless
              motor chug
                          surf washing in white wake
              more deliberate sounds
                                    busy people
                           loafing people
                   the sky is clear
                                  it goes on and on and on . . .
        now close up my pen
                     and follow bird to bow

afternoon

        Now up on bow
                 full of brigade members
                     I begin talking to Marsha
                         when roar goes up
                                  from farther forward
                 "What is it?"
                        "The Conspiracy is innocent of conspiracy!"

21

"But guilty of everything else"
little magical radio device
actually picks up sounds
made in Miami
concerning activities
in Chicago, Illinois!
and 500 North American
cane-cutters
laugh and shout
over long-awaited news
"But I saw that jury!
They're pigs!
Something funny's going on.
All those people
organized around the Conspiracy's innocence
will stop fighting now!"
"No!"
shout others
arguments briefly flare
clarifying details
rise of voices
in political chatter
some Cubans and Puerto Ricans singing Latin songs quietly
as talk subsides
with at least two music sources
and calm sea roar
cut by boat
another source of music
clothes drying
cameras
notebooks
people studying Spanish language
elbow on knees
cheek in hand
rests
others leaning on gigantic spare propeller

                                        propped amid the clutter
                            with hands in pockets
                gently fearful and staring
                                half-looking and listening
                    to everything at once

February 19, early morning — arrival in Havana

5 AM
                    first morning sounds
                            of water running
                    Cuban men in bathroom
            talking softly and excitedly
    As soon as sleepiness made possible
                                slipped out of sleeping bag
                        put on undershirt
                                    blue wrinkled workshirt
                            cheap green army fatigues
                    smelly sweatsocks
                                    and worn workboots
                        taking towel comb and soap
                        below for a piss
                            and water-testing
                                    still cold
            with soap I made do on hands and face
                                    and combed thinning hair
    Now up to my upper bunk
                        to pack spare pants
                                    towel and sweater
                            in sleeping bag
                    with rope device
                            for shoulder-carry sling
        other things with books and notebooks
                                clothespins dirty laundry
                    Whitman Bashō Lévi-Strauss

                    Ashbery Ginsberg
            in Manhattan-bought briefcase
    Finally run up metal stairs
                    to dining room
                            and out on deck
            Havana harbor lights
                    in semi-circle ring
few
                    regularly spaced road lights
                            to complex central vertical thrill
            buildings old and new
                    crumbling castles
                            decadent Hilton
                            of Batista days
            hidden in pre-dawn darkness
            little lights moving along road
                    sign of life
                    in strangely warm air
    A feeling of being within a new culture
                    a day after old Miami culture
            two days after cultureless ocean
            with mythological associations
                            western scientific probes
                                and constellations

Now a city
            Havana
    people there somehow expecting me
                    the bustling across the curving bay
                            somehow part of me
            both alien and intimate
                    like my soul
    Short talk on deck
                    sentences observations
            total inadequacy
                            haze of light over Havana
            where sun will rise

More people straggle on deck
which is soon full
half Cubans half North Americans
our combo
pulls out congas
and bells and sticks
and sings songs we've learned on board
Latin rhythms at home
conga line
bounces through men's dormitory
awakening *brigadistas* with singing and clapping
and dances back on deck
white pennants
with red numbers
for each of 18 brigades on board
waved by dancers
then inside for guava juice
and salami and cheese sandwich!
preparation for our arrival

[Finally we got in at 9 AM, past Moro Castle. People and Cuban brigades met us, also brass Cuban band à la Perez Prado. On buses right away, lots of people in streets waving. One gave me his address asking me to write.

A girl named Max was sitting next to me, very emotionally caught up in the idea — i.e., the reality — of being on socialist soil.

After only about five minutes on the road, during which time we passed through a tollgate without paying any tolls, we stopped right there, on the highway, in back of the five preceding buses, each with its brigade in it, in order to have a snack.

Carol, in our brigade, at one point suggested that we set an example for the other brigades by doing some exercises right then and there, which we did. First, some touching of toes without bending knees, then situps, which I led, then general bending and twisting, and clenching of fists to improve our grips of the machete. That was fun, and by this time

I was feeling closer to the people in my brigade, liking them, not at all jealous of people in "better" brigades, or anything like that. I also felt closer to people in the other brigades. It was just this feeling embodied in the Ashbery quote: "Have you begun to be in the context you feel / Now that the danger has been removed?"

At the camp, Trude, Carol, et al., tried cutting cane and chewed on some.]

CANE

February 21, mid-afternoon

"Incendiary bottles"
in Paris
Granma says
murder of pregnant woman
by ex-sergeant
in North American Southland
mysterious violent country
Radio Havana
English language program
over loud-speakers daily
during midday break
This morning special
"*de pie!*" at 4:45 AM
and breakfast in heavy rain
Why?
Was everyone's watch wrong?
We grunt through meal
what time zone is this?
this rain pisses me off
4:45 every morning?
do we have to cut cane in the rain?
wash up in cold faucet water
piss in comic concrete hole
nearly choking on wire strung across the top of each bathroom booth
neck high
yesterday little pink toilet paper pennants hung as warning
this morning watch out!
wake up
beware
return in protective poncho and straw hat

to tent
with my machete
number 23
from Brigade 6's rack
find someone's file
and begin sharpening edge
not knowing yet if I know correct method
suddenly loud-speaker blare
"Come *campañeros* and greet newly arrived brigade members!"
we wander out to recreation hall surrounding Californians
passing through us one by one
They came by plane from Mexico City
some of them by bus from San Francisco
to Cubana plane
some passionate greetings
then sitting through same speech as yesterday
from Javier Ardizones
camp leader

about 6 AM
sky clearing
wind through big trees over tents
more sharpening of machetes
then form in brigades
and march half awake to fields

February 22, 8:30 PM

Mostly moods
and chaos of sensitive impressions
from silent façades of faces
willing to create one social image or another
from fantasies of how one should relate
to imaginary social reality
Anthropological perspective implies
those within a social entity
can't accurately describe it

and we all have fantasies
about this social entity
not quite yet in existence
even new to Cuba
It isn't Cuba
and it isn't North America
not straightforward as cane-cutting
nor familiar as bourgeois violence
a "culture gap"
between Cuban material exigencies
and US movement intellectual bloodletting
"with a heart of gold"

Swimming in this dream becoming Cuba
inundated by activity after activity
and faces switching from open love
to paranoid contempt
passing each other on red earth
between giant pines and fruit trees
and thick distant planes of cane
amid large thatched community dining and recreation halls
free dentist
armed guard
odor of molasses and partially processed sugar
operable DeSoto
with heavier steel hood
than the past decade's cost-effectiveness permits
all the rattling fifties cars
giving us a certain distance
and sense of nostalgia
we still sometimes don't see each other
don't know how to begin each situation
with the circumstances we find ourselves in
as if this were a talky movement conference
not the *zafra*
de los diez millones

8:45 PM

    The content I'm getting used to
        benches TV movie
               four discussions within my view
          howling wind
       in the movie
             less melodramatic breeze
                   flapping through tents
          there's no time for anything but cane-cutting
and Cuban music on TV
               and I want to concentrate on just one thing
        or everything
      meanwhile a singleminded mosquito
                  got me on my left foot

February 23, 2:30 PM

A little after 5 it's *DE PIE!*
And we get up to start our day
Sharpening our machete blades
For the Venceremos Brigade

(chorus)

Emulation, Emulation
Fuck bourgeois competition
Yeah the Man is in the canefield
Lookin' just like cane

The sun comes up and we cut and pile
Chopping our way right down the aisle
Hey someone's cutting more over there
That's somethin' I just can't bear

I'll chop off the leaves a little lower
Looking for the right spot makes me slower
I won't waste no time clearing the ground
Those roots won't make a sound

(chorus)

Now that cat's being very neat
Chopping at the ground where it's O so sweet

Feburary 24, 2:30 PM

Hot heat
numb thumb
orange tents
canvas-colored tents
hundreds of Americans
dozing midday
the smell of pollen from somewhere
in this ravaged countryside
Think of all the enormous pines
we can encourage to live long lives
when the canefields are cut down
so many no longer needed
no longer enormous plantations
mills
nothing but valleys of trees and streams
sometimes muddy
sometimes clear
small white heron-like birds
landing privately
taking off
in leaps
or hawks floating in circles
with digital feathers spread

comfort in stretching
Tuesday
and I just napped for half an hour
my head on two copies of *Granma*
my back on small gray and rust-colored stones
that fill the tent floor and camp paths
I'm sitting under a fruit tree
some Latin music in the distance
a truck rumbles
gets up speed
another's motor runs standing still
footsteps on pebbles
Still more Americans arrived early this morning
so we were awakened at 4:45 AM
but it was tough
a cramp doubling me up
finally squatting for a shit
my first Cuban diarrhea

Just ate an orange I saved from yesterday morning
the slightly warm juice sweet and natural
little parcels of liquid
in bunches called sections
leaving my hands sticky
Sitting next to a lazy Spanish lesson
Jamy Kevin Jay and Ted
"Me gusto la merienda"
metal can brought to fields by truck
and hauled a hundred yards
with smaller tin of pastries
another with cups
sweet Cuban cola
without carbonation
tasting great by the muddy ditch
between two canefields
This morning
some in our brigade

cut through the field
meeting members of another brigade
chopping from the other side
big smoke from dynamited trees in distance
smaller stream of smoke from ancient train
blowing whistle on the way to the mill
"¿Le gusta a trabajar en los Estados Unidos?"
"No me gusto"
"¿Le gusta a trabajar en Cuba?"
"Si! me gusto!"
hiding in tall cane to take a shit
furry spiders and rats
that leave red spots on cane they chew
the stillness
and reminiscence of urban building
in tall concrete-seeming palm posts
open book keeps face in darkness
second day in the fields
three hours left
exhausted people resting
from vast physical effort
and bad digestion
Now I smell fish or sea water
mild wafting from distant Caribbean
or cooking for this evening already
a breeze rustles leaves
woman's meeting going on somewhere
Soon back to the gray-green piles of cane we stacked
heavy gloves in 3 PM subtropical heat
clean cane
cane cane cane
cramps in my stomach again
"Does anybody here have a file?"

(A Cuban member of the brigade passes by
followed by a militia man
carrying two tape recorders over his shoulder

He stops when he sees me writing a poem
and asks me if it's about the brigade
and I explain this task I've set myself)

This man here is filing his machete
this man here is reading an economics book
these four men are having a Spanish lesson
those in the distance are laughing and talking
sounds of metal scraping metal
a woman's laugh effused from tent
someone has energy to explain something
in another tent
I'm playing with stones
At the mill warehouse
two enormous conical piles of raw yellow-brown sugar
conveyor belts
something like flour filling the empty spaces

February 25, about 2 PM

Last night I was
O so tired
but my back's leaning on a bunk
through tent canvas wall
wind billowing through
someone comes by in moccasins
"I was telling everybody
that the shit's gonna hit the fan pretty soon"
come back from morning cutting
finding tent graffiti
of a perverse nature
"Off the people!"
"Off women!"
"Viva diarrhea!"

"Seattle sucks!"
and others in a similar vein
"Whose machete is sharper?
Mine or yours?"
"Some places mine.
Some places yours."
"MINE is sharper! . . . hahaha . . .
cough cough cough!"
There must be some agents around
a change of linen
while we were out this morning
a refreshing shower coming back
early morning mist means hot day
big metal jaws
lifting cane piles
dumping them in trailer
tractor motors beside us all morning
driven by dark-haired kids
We broke through
meeting a California brigade at 8:30 AM
coming from the other side
Two women
wondering why they didn't break through in their rows
one takes a look
comes back saying
"That much to go!
and it's a woman too
would you believe it!"
Eye protection warnings passed around
Kevin's eye hurt by cane leaf
I'm sitting on a light blue pillow
back from lunch
I am 99% self-disciplined already
I show up for all the Spanish lessons
that don't take place

I'm doing something all the time
tossing pebbles in the path
thinking of the sunset
In the canefields
my partner says
"I was thinking about how I could keep my kids
from becoming revisionists"
My mind goes blank
or wanders from stalk-image to stalk-image
hiding in the long slick leaves
trying to see the "trees"
instead of the "forest"
What's going on in Boston?
it's snowing
this afternoon
we're gonna cut some "heavy" *arrobas*
A climbing frog on wall of men's john
at 5:30 AM
dark green
suction cups on toes
decides to jump on the dark
leaf-strewn ground
my sweatband gets a darker red
heavy with sweat
I'm hot and tired
dripping and itching
hands getting harder
I have a fantasy of an elephant squirting iced root beer
as I let a thin tube of water
fall from the clay jar
a few inches in air
to the back of my throat
Someone's being criticized in the next tent entrance
and she's reacting defensively
told she's hard to take
bourgeois tendencies
dogmatism

defeatism
by "nice guys"
It would be nice to be able to stand back
from scenes like these
and discuss
whether people need criticism
in this institutionalized form
Now they're playing with their machetes
great game of competitive insight goes onward
spray some *Populares cigarros* with pebbles
release your aggressions cutting cane

February 27, 2 PM

I feel
a cool breeze
in my VB shirt
colored orange
the VB color
my phlegm red
a deep red
from antiseptic liquid
squirted down the back of my throat
I'm feeling great
the only anxiety
no people coming around any more
persisting in spite of apparent
impossibility of loneliness
though some people turn me off
but I don't hate them
some people snub me
and I should remind them
"You shouldn't do that!"
not to be ready to come here
to learn what we can learn

the sick people
vomiting over doctor
sitting down reading Marx and Engels
Selections
try-outs
for the brigade volleyball team
no form of competition acceptable
"I'm working until the *merienda!*"
alone in the field of stacked "dirty" cane
we cut
emulating Reynaldo Castro
who came by
to exhibit his style
static on PA speaker I don't mind
The Voice of Vietnam
Western music
with a touch of the East
the paddies
the temples
swordplay
Run Run Shaw
from Hong Kong
the capital of which is Victoria
big multi-trunk trees
sap oozing out
big echo on radio news recording
of speech from some hall
demonstration at Carbondale
demonstration in LA
one in San Francisco
and Boston
and DC
an American prisoner in North Vietnam
the theme music
slurs to a stop
sabotage?

or bad technician
                    slipping in a *merienda*
or rushing out to the fields
                    for volunteer work
"Work is work!"
        revolutionary assumption
            another big blue sky
low clouds in the morning
            so cold
            little pink or violet wires
                        to lights
                strung in trees
            for illumination
        clothes drying in daytime clear thereness
        congas and flute
                    I am beginning to be patient
                        in a revolutionary sense
enjoying Cuba
        and my fantasies of pulling rank when I return home
                    ropes
                    in primitive tension
        clotheslines part of the tent-being
                        big issues absorbing people
                    like racism
                male chauvinism
                elitism
                        not to mention communism
        my friends in Havana
                            I'm not jealous of anybody
                    or that hawk
        who I become in my mind
                        cloud like a puff of smoke
                a guy blowing smoke rings in waiting room
                            of medical building
prescription line
            or waiting to see the doctor

the day's *Granma* out yet?
what's the big news?
what shall we talk about?
I'm willing to be more sensitive
than I have been
less defensively assertive
wondering
also if she thinks I hate her
changed my clothes
this afternoon
should wash underwear
I don't care about that
like the frog out of place on wall of john
or spoiled human puppy
loafing around
in a revolutionary human land
I absorb this routine
like Kleenex absorbs faster and faster
an attractive limp
thin legs
nice cotton dress
indeterminate light color
red bandanna
black hair
plastic frames
strange pretty lips
confident LA style
lots of women wearing same
blue balloon blouse
Cuban issue no doubt
Kunstler in Santa Barbara
a riot ensues
O to be a big issue
the first machete charge
brilliant *Mambises*
from Oriente

Foreign Relations Ministry makes me nervous
even in Cuba
"Imagine *us* running the country!"
Haven't thought much of other poets for a while
but Louis MacNeice comes to mind
dark drug New England winter house I left
everything drearily becoming academic
so I should stand on my toes more
to protest waste of paper
Cuban birds flutter like scrawny wren
I'll know when it's time to become homesick
a headline in *Juventud Rebelde*
we get all the words
but it still makes no sense
sun behind a fleecy cloud
I want to get away from pure temporal moods

*

Night before last
meeting mysteriously called
I knew nothing about
but overheard dinner conversation
reference to
all-white meeting tonight
Later after brushing teeth
accidentally ran into
large crowd in front of
blank billboard
in heated argument
One guy strutting
putting on rock star act
saying meeting unnecessary
Others saying
cut the shit
Third World asked us to create

some communication channel
to them
what's so hard about that?
Sectarian gabbling
infinite frustration
we gotta deal with all the
camp's problems

*

                    I didn't know
            what the fuck they were talking about
        discussing formal organization
                            or need for it
                I guess people's good intentions
                                can't be taken for granted
                self-discipline
            confused with authority
                                of leader or institution
        refusal to discuss reality
                    immediate leap to vague abstractions
                                mystifications
                        axes to grind
        my impulse is to say
                Fuck it
            I came here to cut cane
                        so I'll ignore people who annoy me
                            and just get down to work
                but that's the deficient way
                        I've acted in the past
                no longer acceptable
                            current imperative
                                to articulate my perspective
                    I keep telling this to myself
            and it somehow doesn't feel real
                        reality to me

consists of people and places
problems arising on secondary level
alien from immediate circumstances
people not "communicating" anyway
except on one-to-one level
or in small groups
How do you institutionalize
mass intimacy
except with tribal music experience
or thousands of eyes focused on leader
or movie screen?
popcorn would be better than parliament or bureaucracy
"You whites have got to get your shit together!"
what are the objective conditions?

February 28, 2:15 PM

Air flavored with smoke
and wind blowing
gusts of talk
billow into yelling
with gusts of wind
a strange walk
arms swung from elbows
lifted from knuckles
legs hidden by arm movement
she gets along anyway
attractive plain pale face
I'm unhappy now
except with the climate
and the weekend of sleep and beach ahead
I don't have the clothes here to keep up my image
my hair is too short
the sky is northern
which brings back memories

                               it's the end of a workweek
            like it always has been
                    in America
            why should I feel differently?
    to fill myself up with beer
                and heavy food to regret!
                            infinite mobility
                    within a two-mile radius
                                filled with friends
            and countless self-indulgences
        on credit
                        ripping off pens movies spices
    sun in continual haze of sophistication
            and all the dope you crave
                    under light signs and car roar
        cultural revolutionary
                        decadent technological west
    birds a design
            on building wall

[Found out that one of new poems is missing, 6 pp. one from 2/20.
Don't know what happened yet. Am suspicious of everyone. . . . Saw
beginning of music "cultural" evening. Later, saw the Bravos Brothers
and Ignacio Villa "Bolo de Nieve" (Snowball), the pride of Cuba.]

March 1, at the beach mid-afternoon

            The sea through pines
                limpid ink
                        flowing on sea surface
                    or under
                            from squid
                                mysteriously cold and bubbly
            at beach

formerly belonging to Dupont or Batista
or newly developed
by Revolution
"Baptiste! Baptiste!"
less sacred
than the cinema mime

*

Nine hours sleep
felt strange
awake at 7 AM
slow breakfast
feeling distant
not to get involved in Sunday leisure
before month more of cane
still feel stigma
of yesterday's stolen poem
I wrote it on February 20th
and it's gone this first of March
Am I to blame?
25 blue and beige buses
at beach parking lot
seen through low young coconut palms
brought us here
slow old Cuban rock music
young hen pumps neck and tiny head across thick prickly grass
bayoneted Batista grass
in food search
Are my friends avoiding me?

*

Buses rumble down palm aisles
earth dusty red
past last century's sugar mill

                              wooden factory art
       we wave to people in towns and on farms
                          and some wave to us
                     a calf sees us
                                   its elders don't
                                       or ignore us

March 2, after 8 PM

                          Yesterday
                     on yellow film
                                   a previously undeveloped beach
                          green
                     with chickens and coconuts
                                   on buses
                          sand
              rocks shells sponges
                          spinets
                     violin Cuban jazz
                     her dancing learning
                                   "I'll never learn!"
              Book Committee tonight
                     eight hours work
                          many *arrobas*
              more than we expected
                                   caking our mouth
                          silver spies
                     jugs of water
                          drip down shirts
                                   hard pressed
              anger at neighbor
                     competitor
                     cane over wire-like grass and flower runners
       oxen grazing grotesquely
                                   Overhead

low sky
missing sun
not in eyes' today
ant thinly crosses gray table
the ant is dark brown-blood red
and quick
I blow it backwards once
then off the table
I think
it returns
as one reporter leaves
off his expense account
politics
sad
depressed
glimmer of hope
note of presence
manipulative chatter
intimidation
vanilla ice cream
the beach
chunks of sand
I pass by her reading and once writing
"scribbling"
piano scales in the afternoon
crossing volleyball court
to ping pong table
for *Granma*
got into a game
violated by wind
balls scatter
line to hand in laundry
Antonioni desolation
descending scales
I must write a letter
sad news

McCarthyism anew
I read Whitman on bus back from beach
                    as some danced to tape of old Little Richard
        to new Stones
            pass by school
                    children lining road
                        beautiful

    sisal
            west into sunset
                    others read
                played recorder
        one came over
            sat beside me on grass to play
                    coconuts fell in branchful
                        in wind

        scramble for them
            "in love"
                    depressed
        as usual
                not in love
                    depressed as usual
            Cuba mild
    cold winter
                words quit typing rhythm
        static noise
            drops acid
        takes a doze
                    cleans his mental closet
            full of skeletons
                    generations
                Socialist camp in '30s
        poetry of '30s
                floods
        from Russia
                    four-wheel drive trucks
            drive through States

bad news
                alienation
                meaning in work
                        "work is work"
                today we all cut
        tomorrow we all pile
                        some of us are tired
                                some are very tired
                        I drop defenses
            like coconuts
                        personal poetry
                what happened
        in 1895?
                what's happening here?
            I'll write that letter
            crying nymphs
                        Happy Birthday
                congas
                        scales
        chatter
                maps
                sisal
            bus tired up highway hill
                        cows
                    kids
                impressive
                    alone at the beach
tiny coconut
            pine cones
            Cuban kids on seesaw
            "Hola!"
                    from me on rusted playground ride
shells
        rum and cola
                beer for lunch
                        cerveza

           with hamburger
                    beans and rice and yucca
    shadow of a nose
       on wall
         say the destructive thing
sky supporting vultures
        shadows shades
    into myself
       woo-oo
     fall outward
  blowing across bottle top
            slow downward scales on piano
        benches set up for meeting

March 4, afternoon

      Weakness all week
   I enjoy the present midday pleasantness
            all people tired and not moving fast
          in front of my eyes
      wrote exhausted incoherent letter yesterday afternoon
     what's my name?
  what am I doing here?
      this is hard work!
         I don't want to return to the fields
          for four more hours of work this afternoon
    but I'll do it

   somehow I know I'll do it
   I must be a coward
   and can't give up the idea
   that I'm an effete dilettante
   broad like an elm leaf
   collectivized chinese pine needles

WORK!
                    yiiich!

                    typical gringo attitude
            it should always be a quarter to one
                            as long as
                    I have access to this shade
                at least my cold's disappearing

                              *

            Evviva! Evviva!
    smile
            so difficult
                    moving difficult
            a pain in this pinky
                        and complementary one in the other
                    sympathetic pain
            if I don't think about it
                            I don't fuck myself up as much
        dirty uncomfortable person
                        should I be neat and get a haircut?
            Cuban barber
                            for free
    vanish in crackling pebbles
                    I shaved and shat and showered
                            now to dirty myself up again
        what a brew!
                5 or 6 more weeks left
                        then big Cuban vacation
        from the Isle of Youth
                    to the Sierra Maestre

at night

Blister bliss
front of crisp
mosquito attack
hurt tip of finger
right on up to here
ecstasy of body pain
out in the fields again
don't bother me
in my repellent gestures
6–12
by Union Carbide
no back to chair
weights to lift
hurts my wounds
"Just kind of ignore 'em"
a single loud cricket
easily readable
personable feeling for her
out in the fields again
bug on me
"bug out"
"hippy out"
"cop out"
Cubans first in Central American
and Caribbean Games
held in Panama
an old toothpaste
front for the mafia
none here
instead there's cane
and male chauvinism
macho
mucho macho
who understands whom?

Orion pissing in the cloudless night sky
no yellow lights
lack of neon
laughing at us behind our backs
the Russians are doing better
so are the Bulgarians
not to mention the North Koreans
ask me to type anything
and I'll do it
for money
individuals full of Darvons
or medicated rum
on prescription
for personal migraine uptightness telegram
no phone to Habana
but phone New York?
Boston?
London?
Moscow?
sure
just sign up in the information tent
and we'll call you by PA
those pinkies hurt

*

Got very tired Tuesday morning
cutting cane
came back to camp
and got on lunchline
talked with new-found friend
and departed after tiny cup of coffee
to the loudspeaker under the movie screen
casting shadow
in which people coolly sat
listening to Radio Havana

over the movie theater speaker
"provoking panic in several persons"
sun still and tropic
standing in it
then sitting down on palm log bench
for rest of newscast
occasional weak cheers
in defensive audience
finally slowly drifted back to tent
slouched on bunk
What should I do
so tired this siesta hour?
thinking as I talked to Joy
I have a friend at Radio Havana
deep toneless American voice
speaking editorial on Laos
only tones seeping through tent canvas
what's your position?
slouching
untying shoelaces on mudcaked workboots
$2 + 2 = 4$
THAT'S ROBERT'S VOICE!
Tell me what I should do!
Long shot
run outside
shoes unlaced
full of weird excitement
searching for disembodied distant
speaking voice
person behind it
camera way up in fruit tree
hard brown fruits thrown down
milky sap where stem pulled off
it tastes awful
big black seeds

I tell a few people
    Carol, Lucy
              who wants to visit with Robert and Meg
                    on Havana free day
          repetition
        fruit falling slow motion
  blue blue sea
           bright green cabbages
       no soundtrack
A Man Is A Woman
                French New Wave-y film
         Brechtian epic didacticism
              harsh primary colors
     international style
         tell someone
can I call Havana from here?
       No
    only New York or Boston or . . .
             man runs after volleyball
                  in dark camp background
     sound of dominoes shuffled
      falling
  in Southeast Asia
       Latin America
   my mind
      I'm not thinking
       I thought
   I don't have to think
        so I'm not thinking
  this just flows over me
     even my depressions
    a feeling of safety
         sharp machete whacks
     on fleshy head
    disorientation of sensibility

          listening to star beeps
             in nightfields
                        sweet-smelling cane
                  blue flickering star
   capitalist needs
             hangups
          unearthed
                 floating freely
            I don't have to think
                       because I'm acting
        cutting cane
                uneasy nights of sleep
                    can't get to sleep
awake
    or tired
             Robert's editorializing voice
                floats in circles
           a big brother
    in deep
           red lights under red tent canvas roof
               I love the unacceptable avant-garde
      tears of Christ
            or Buddha mouth
          in inexpressible period
               void
            breath
voided by runny nose
         avoiding the actual
                I'm not thinking
    cane is alive too
       so what am I gonna do?
            cry over each slashed stalk?
what does "not thinking" mean?
     no more arctic head struggles
               I moved south

March 5, afternoon

"Comrade Mela Morf
                        please come to the telegraph office"
                                The Book Committee
                                        now has its own tent
        behind the building
                on the porch of which
                        the chess games are played
                "Everybody who signed up
                        to either submit material
                                photographs
                                        or journals
                                                etc.
                or to work with the committee
                        should come to the tent tonight"
        a small brown dog
                climbs over my leg to inspect typewriter
                wanders off
                what wind
        the hottest part of the day
                annoying paper flap
                                morning work clothes drying
                my fingers strong
                        big clouds sometimes hiding sun
                                In the fields
                        my hat flies off all the time
        I put it down
                under a heavy stalk of cane

                                *

        "Play with me!"
                says the puppy
                        running his paws through someone's hair
        "What long hair!"

                              says the short-haired Cuban dog
                          feeling low
                              right leg tired
                  three and a half days of hard work this week
                              almost doubled last week's daily output
          "We're in first place!"
                              something that doesn't exist
                  "male chauvinist competitive bullshit"
                          can't help feeling a twinge of pleasure
          but should figure out the reason for it
                              to see if it's justified
                          or complacent crime
                                      "non-struggle"
                  maybe it just proves we tried

March 9, afternoon

          "Hi!"
          some food is stuck just outside my mouth
          I caught a chameleon out in the fields
          I'm going to tell you about a dream
          A fighter pilot dropping a heavy load over Laos
          A solar eclipse glimpsed through two Polaroid lenses
          March 8th
          The International Day of Women
          Tania la Guerrillera millionaire brigade of women
          cutting cane with the Venceremos Brigade
          on the International Day of Women
          Out in the fields
          clouds
          clearing just enough for solar eclipse viewing
          in crowds around tents
          examining some *pica-pica* through camera lenses
          Cubans playing dominoes on table next to mine
          "Hi!"

later

                            Fish
                              eggs
                                bacon
                    herons
                        gliding into fields
                                            landed aristocracy
                            no comment
                let us play
                    getting to know you better
                                    if this isn't politics
                                    what is?!
bleeding or sweating green through headband
                    got to get this together
                                        or read more Whitman
                            who I read on bus back from beach
                                        and at beach also
                        I feel like I'm sitting too low to type well
                        and my wrists itch
                                    and that doesn't help
                in general the conditions for writing this poem
                gravitate toward the troublesome end of the spectrum

                            A girl in a yellow scarf
                            is posing for a sketch
                            holding up her machete
                            The artist puts her curly dark hair
                            in two sets of long locks
                            over her breasts
                            She has a serious Russian tractor look
                            and she knows I'm looking at her
                            Russian tractor romance

                    Mass open tent
                    but I have trouble opening my eyes

keeping them open in sunlight
and noise of dominoes is killing me

＊

I want to live a long time
and find out what's going to happen
I seem for the moment
to know almost every American
who passes by this table
"Hi!"
"Hi!"
"Hi!"
"Hi!"
"Hi!"
"Hi!"
"Hi!"
"Hi!"

The sketch done
model leans on plaster wall
small breasts on big body
under orange brigade teeshirt
looks at sketch
she and artist walk off

I look at vultures soaring long distances
my mind goes with them
and I can't hear the dominoes shuffled

A lone nail sticks from
timber post
of veranda

fingers at the end of wings

"I Sing the Body Electric"
"Starting from Paumanok"
"Spontaneous Me"
"From Pent Up Aching Rivers"
"A Woman Waits For Me"

The great melange continues in time
O Walt
the ball keeps rolling
like rumors

around 9 PM

This is impossible
whatever happened yesterday
is gone
Like a turpentine porcupine
dancing around vacant circus tents

"I used to be in the circus
before I joined the movement"

Impossible
distance
to the cane
far past the mill
muddy roads
I can write whatever I want to
but these aren't lies
the Temptations' *Greatest Hits*

A cable to Europe
a big "O"
drawn to the *centro de acopio*
I like you green shawl

dragging your feet
in love
drag
in drag
in love
loving your feet
you big ugly clodhoppers

Jumping across bouncy fallen cane leaves
momentum built up to muddy road
so oops! I fall
that red mud over my shoes cuffs sleeves
the water jug I put on ground for balance
"You better slow down!"

later at night

R. leaves for home
on Friday
without telling anyone in brigade in advance
On Saturday
a brigade of women *macheteras*
Tania la Guerrillera
cuts cane with us
six of them with Brigade 6
Then there is a partial solar eclipse
Sunday is International Day of Women
and we go to the beach
it rains on and off all day
and I get drunk on two rum and cola drinks
and read Whitman on the bus on the way home

*

They do everything together
here they are together again

*

A small plane
            with tons of firepower
    is flying over Laos
                R.'s father is shot down
                            missing
    In Cuba R. is cutting cane
        as part of the Venceremos Brigade
            and gets a telegram
                from his girlfriend
    He hasn't spoken to his family for a year

March 10, afternoon

                Calmness detracts
                        from wanted chaos
                    in the mind
        put in a switch
                to tune me out
                    diffuse the rational line
                            until I return
calm in my room
    to ventilate
        with reason
            mental flooding
        from wide experience

                Texaco

        This is the Voice of Vietnam
        This is the Voice of Vietnam

            Heroic Vietnamese women singing
                        the noise is annoying me

and I unbend my legs
                  still intensely distracted
                           National Anthem of the Democratic
                                          Republic of Vietnam
        I think sex is on my mind

later

                  This morning
                        we came across
                           a small meadow
                                    filled with low-growing tomatoes
                        some grass
                              I took a piss
                                    and scared a small lizard
                              which ran up a stalk of cane
            Later
        I got a stomach cramp
                  and took a shit there
                        in idyllic surroundings
                              light and shadow through leaves
                                    in grass that lay down
            I pulled my pants down
            slight tingling on my ass and prick
                  and the yellow-brown
                              cream cheese textured shit
                                    effused
                        with smooth controlled aid of bowel muscles
                  and lay in peanut butter glop
                              in grassy light
        I am sleeping now
            only the yellow toilet paper betrays my humanness
                        I cover it up with a large fuzzy tomato leaf

later

The first day
of machete sharpening
with noisy electricity
hum grind
the feel of the wheel
of the cramp in my stomach
the noisy music from the speaker above me
"What time is it?"
it must be time to leave
my fingers and back will tire
and the long walk back
weaken me more
voices harmonize
Walt Whitman
a hole in the canvas
compulsion
waxes and wanes
with tiredness
and sloppy graffiti mural we did
not me though
people are too busy
my body is too busy
while asleep too
the news passes by
a famous song over the speaker
all our music is folk music
grass growing on roof
what do I have to say or think
that isn't undisciplined like this?
my mind
should I accept it the way it is?
have I lost my reason?
my motivation?
should I resolve making days

                    empty of writing
             to spring back wells
                                    of interest
                                        fervor
                    and other shit like that??
        a poem
        of a country
                    a world
                    or planet
                            or the universe
             religion and its importance
                            the guy who fainted in the fields this morning
        thinking then writing
                    I still must break out
                    I'm not interested in starting
                                    to sharpen my machete
             or washing clothes
                            my obligations
                    no letters
I might just get a haircut

[Late to work in afternoon. Very slow cutting. Newer, worse cane. Cuban kid around with slingshot shooting tomatoes. Played baseball with tomatoes and bat of cane with kid who was better than me. Long walk home.]

March 13, early morning

                    Looking out over fields at 8 AM
             after intense rain an hour ago
                            kept us from cutting this morning
                    people equivocally happy
                            reasons to be

glad or sad
chance to flood the early morning
with vision
instead of body movement and strain
dampness and birds
not postponed perceptions
the clouds or mist
seeping through your awakening
as in capitalist luxury back home
an hour or two of Maxim freeze-dried coffee
maybe some oatmeal
reading the latest issue of local underground paper
or book you can concentrate on
orange juice
luxury
private bathroom out in the hall
the pleasant slums
all the people to help
not going back to parents' china knick-knacks
and thick carpets
an uneven line of palms
and dark green and tan tents
some yellow or orange too
hallway
five-floor walkup
upstate New York
the Cascades
Vermont
Canada
beautiful summer weekends
luxury cans of gourmet foods
level mist
the clouds separating
profound shape
luxury

for everyone
when we don't work
waste time
look at trees
aesthetic things
muddy roads beautiful
when you don't get your feet muddy walking on them
birds punctuating silence
put some classical French music
on the turntable
to have a front room!
beautiful streams of runoff running in ditches
people running in packs on St. Mark's Place
or Telegraph Avenue
I read a book
it's a novel
the characters live in London
others have vast lands in Russia
a home in the Midi
own a factory in the American northeast
St. Paul society
San Francisco culture
Back Bay architecture
the expressway runs through the slums
destroying sections
dividing the rest
it's a tragedy
someone with good intentions
fucks up
and finally dies
while the world rolls on
luxuriantly
like a tragedy
a death-like diamond you hid
when the revolution came

I don't like preparing
                    for the coming holocaust
        but I'm preparing for something
                    the playful floodlights
                                clacking dominoes
            a small patch of weeds
                                    old stone foundation

                            *

        Last night
            smoking part of smelly Cuban cigar
                    typing an essay on Women's Liberation
                            by Third World male brigade member
                    for the Book Committee
        disturbed by point of view
                wondering what best way to respond would be
                        agreeing white movement
                            is largely unserious and adolescent
        but feeling present confusion
                necessary stage to future maturity
                        resenting essayist's condescension
                            and lack of generosity and understanding
                was woman he spoke with representative?
                            etc.

[More bombings in NYC.]

March 14

[Sharpened machete, dressed and left to go to new field, across road
from Aguacate. Talked with Eva on the way. She asked me to dedicate
today's cutting to her father, 75 years old, earned $3000 this year as jan-
itor, the most in his life, "pulled himself up by his bootstraps." Cut very
well, 7 enormous piles. Long walk home.]

March 16, afternoon

I just handed a Vietnamese a fork
as a symbolic gesture
of my willingness
to help him get his utensils
so he could eat
grow strong and healthy
and continue to struggle against
American imperialism
in the Vietnamese selva
He graciously and shyly accepted the fork
and passed it to a comrade of his
the forkless one
until I came along
They and the other Vietnamese
sat down by the entrance to the dining hall
and ate their food
I went my own way
to another part of the hall
heart-warmed and hungry
sat down by myself
swallowed spoonful after spoonful of soup
dipping a roll in it
picking up tan garbanzos
mixing rice with egg/potato/meat salad
finishing it up
and eating sweet pineapple sauce
a cup of water
brought metal multi-recessed dish
to rear of hall
and after sipping small cup of strong sweet coffee
returned to tent

*

On long line outside of dining hall
          waiting to get in to eat
          I spotted Eva
       sauntering up to the infirmary
          with a roll
                she's taking in to Joe who's there
        right away she came out again
           and sat nearby on palm log seat
              of movie theater
              looking over her shoulder
    restless
      as if told to wait
  gentle arrogance of
            "*I* know what I'm doing here"
      in the face of the mystery
    "maybe I should be someplace else?!"
Where are all the people in this camp?

March 16, afternoon, and March 18, evening

      The Vietnamese are supposed to arrive at 2 PM
      I wake up between 7 and 8 in the morning
put on workboots and walk out to canefields
              with Walt Whitman's poems in my hand
        I stop hundreds of yards
    from men working picking up piles of cane
        with hydraulic
             but frail-looking claws
       and dumping them into trailing carts
and there I recite aloud
      in early morning literary tones
        "Song of the Redwood Tree"
       a California song
           about the new generations

rising from the beautiful landscape
the same moment
a dying redwood
is fallen in dusty light
by men
who hear not the song
Walt Whitman hears
Uncertain if I hear it too
I wander back to camp
trying to think about
Cuban/American culture gap
"buenas dias" to armed guard
wander around tent and camp environs
until 10 AM meeting
with others in Brigade 6
to execute Will's idea for poster greeting
for Vietnamese —
red machetes instead of stripes
on US flag
producing waving effect
and black fists instead of stars
spelling out "VB"
in field of
postponed aesthetic decisions
We set up three benches in sun
outside of Recreation Hall
place large cardboard on it
search around for equipment
paints
which I produce from Book Committee tent cache
where Los Siete de la Raza posters were silkscreened
last night
placed in discarded guava jars
dumped outside of kitchen
red and black

but no brushes
other stuff from personal cache of marking pens and razor blades
and machete #23
One draws rough proportions
another makes machete template
from spare cardboard
another a stencil of tiny stylized fist
Thing fits together
people come by
admiring
others not able to make out what the fists spell
or otherwise signify
"That looks like a television set"
"Stand back 20 feet!"
"I don't know. What is it?"
"Whose idea was that?"
I say
"Will's"
he says "Joel's"
"Will's"
"Joel's"
"Will's"
"Joel's"
"Everybody'll look at that and say
The Old Mole!"
"*Stop* it!"
"Even the Vietnamese
will recognize the style"
Just in time
we finish masterpiece
and I hold it by the side of the road
we all line up in single file
waiting beyond 2 PM for the Vietnamese to arrive
Someone else holds poster while I piss in
everpresent cane

everyone takes my picture
finally blue soundtruck speeds towards us
blaring signal of awaited arrival
two or three black cars turn distant dusty corner
and move in our direction
we await with greater discipline each moment
clutching freshly picked tough wildflower bouquets
posters and cameras
wearing yellow red and blue bead rings
and Vietcong flag headbands
same flag painted on straw hats
ancient Detroit Imperials
flow through us with shiny chrome
like tanks in victory parade
"Ho Ho Ho Chi Minh
the NLF is gonna win"

*

We run after cars into camp
camp PA speaker
says
"Let's take the Vietnamese comrades
to the Recreation Hall!"
and we run to parking lot
and escort these ten small smiling men
the fifty yards to thatched
low-gabled hall
without walls
hundreds standing on benches
waving machetes
and posters
to the few passing to the front
the major speakers and their personal translators
take their places

and we stand for national anthems
of Cuba
Democratic Republic of Vietnam
and South Vietnam
I wonder if the "Star Spangled Banner" will follow
and what would ensue if it did
but it doesn't
and we silently sit down
to hear brief repetitious speeches
from the DRV ambassador to Cuba
a youth leader
and an NLF freedom fighter
each with his own translator
then an endless question period
"What percentage of the South
can safely be said to be liberated?"
I look through darkness
at Cuban silkscreens of Vietnam
hung for the occasion
very colorful
reminding me of popular Japanese prints
the *36 Views of Mt. Fuji*
"Are any American soldiers who deserted
fighting with the NLF?"
Will becomes restless and sits by wall post
playing with black puppy
"What is the status of Vietnamese relations
with the Soviet Union and China?"
Eva wanders in and out
finally closing her eyes in sun sitting by outside wall
"Could you clarify the 5th point
of the Pathet Lao?"
Elizabeth sitting with poster she drew
helmet and bouquet of flowers
"Vigilancia"

"What do you think the Venceremos Brigade should do
when it returns to the United States?"
questions answered in bunches
tediously and repetitiously
Finally I go out
into increasingly cold evening
wander slowly to take piss and wash up
and return to hall
while freedom fighter from the South
is describing how he and his battalion
temporarily took an American airfield
destroying planes
and other materiel
and killing ten officers in a bunker
Immediately long line forms
for late *merienda*
and small groups surround each Vietnamese
on grassy and concrete spaces
asking more personal questions
"Those Vietnamese are a real heavy number!"
back in tent
Everyone destroyed the meditative thought
the meditative fact
that we were all together
cutting cane for the thoughtful Cubans
drowned in "question period" nonsense
and communal boredom

March 17, afternoon

Resting in the field
soft   hard
my machete hand weary
my head weary and thoughtless

my body altogether weary
so I don't know if I can try hard anymore today
tent billows up with wind
funny I don't feel a breeze
God doesn't like me
news weary on speaker
speaker of news weary
Everybody weary
my style weary
my stomach cramps just don't make it
Since I'm in Cuba I must convince myself
that I'm not weary
or that it's psychosomatic
and I must struggle with myself
but I'm too weary

*

N. phones her husband
to see what's up
"What's the financial situation?"
"Pretty good!
I just started divorce proceedings"

*

Someone mysteriously dies by bomb or gas in New York
former friend of his down here
Has she heard about it yet?

[Heard over radio that Ted Gold killed in NY in bomb blast. Went over
to show poem about Eva to Eva.]

March 18, afternoon

In a new canefield late this morning
across the road from the *centro de acopio*
near the mill
lots of rotten stalks
dead leaves filling up spaces
roots away from us
as we advance
our brigade *jefe* comes by down the road
Will shouts to him
"*Renato, este caña* shits!
¿Sabe la palabra inglés
'shits'?"

*

Led Zeppelin
Beatles
Nina Simone
BS&T
Rolling Stones
Sly and the Family Stone
coming over the speakers

Erik Satie

Cuban music

*

Rumors circulating around camp
about plans for us back in the States
Senator asks that our citizenship be taken away
Gusanos attack returned brigade members
we're accused of bombings

in New York City
they say we get guerrilla training in Cuba
the president himself promises to get us
over nationwide TV
I plan to write a book to raise defense costs
in case we get busted

later

Getting overcome again
this time with heat
but I want to get out of it
because I feel more serious about
current situation
vis-à-vis
Venceremos Brigade
what with all the news coming from the States
and melodramatic rumors spreading
over sleepy camp
all the people out to get us
accusing us of all sorts of things
from bombings to being in the service of another government
and I haven't been thinking too seriously
about the meaning of this situation
and all it implies
both for the present
and the delirious future
For me it's been a fairly personal trip
not having been so close to so many people
since I can remember
with literally hundreds of potential lifelong friends
hundreds of potential loves
and an infinity of possible tasks to carry out
once I return to the States
so I should be serious

                    though I have been anyway
            only not like lots of others here
                                locked in narrow political grip
            of rhetoric
                        or secure in their self-indulgence

    I have a hard time keeping track of all the people I meet
                though I'm trying my best
                            asking names
                                    tent and brigade numbers
                    easy too for me to fall in love
                        ten times over
            the people and the cane
                        and our relations with the Cubans
                        preoccupy me
            and I take the future political commitment for granted
                won't know specifically what to do
                        until sometime after I return to the States
                                (I'll think more
                                and write more later)

evening

                    Havana in my mind
            out in the canefields
                            ugliness
                    without trees
                                clean water
                2000 head of cattle
            eating hay in small pens
            alongside the mill
                        I got to get this straight
                            all the priorities
            what to do first

next
package to get around customs
to wash
what I need
get out in the fields again
Eva tired of collective living
Lourdes and Dulce
going back to school
tomorrow morning
10 PM party for them tonight

March 22, night

Set your own house in order
before you go checking up on your neighbor
said "that heavy cat"
Jesus Christ
and I'm sweating from every pore
in a night of pain
full of blasé pleasure
knowing I'll have nothing to regret in the morning
under the collapsed fabric of my tent
a five-minute nap produces a nightmare
waking up
looking over to where Eva naps
on upper bunk
when she moves
I tap her on the shoulder
She's moving in with us in tent 15
because "it's cooler in here"
though it's really gotten warmer
sweating in our sleep
We slice an orange with sleeping Mike's machete
slowly walk through camp

to women's tent
she looks everywhere but at me
when she talks
lifelong study of people
I call it
wanting to be in love
pain and longing
infrequent unremitting touching
arm and sweatband
couched in esoteric terms
I walk alone between coffee plants
under mango trees
painted white chest high
with chemically treated paint
view colonies of tiny spiders
in ivory-colored
clusters of bodies
in middle of single web
which I touch . . .
. . . they move outward
moving seeds
fisheggs
takes me away from lunch at Niña Bonita
artificial insemination
cattle breeding center
cerveza
ham and cheese sandwich
green mangoes falling from trees
water spraying from pipeline joints
guilt if we return to Russian-made truck for seconds
tiny green beans on coffee plants
someone now singing "Suzanne" in camp
a new stage
two weeks of cutting left
beginning not to want it to end

                              until the crisis occurs
                    all static sets of conditions lead to
                       in circles I frequent

                                        *

"To a Stranger"
          by Walt Whitman
             expresses much of what I would like to say
                    about relationships in the *campamento*
                         fucking each other in our minds
                              countless fallings in love
                    dreams of bodies
                    eyes dreaming
                       on another
                                   anxiety
             over the stranger in each of us
There are bodies of certain men here I'd like to touch
          and women with perfect mouths
                              innocent and attentive
I'm too inhibited to name names
          and there are many whose names I don't know
                    but many know how I feel
                         and I know how that adhesiveness
                              exists between two
             cannot be solitary and unreflected
             sensuous bodies
                              consciousness and dreams
          under trees
                    in tent bunks
                         dressing and undressing
                    eating food
                              looking to others
                                   at other dining hall tables
                    discussing almost anything in groups

falling in love many times a day
                    "That's interesting, man —
                              Love for the masses!"
the discipline of doing what you want to do
          whether the revolution
                         is a dream or a nightmare
              or present history
     "For each man kills the thing he loves"
                         converting hatred into energy
               collective gash of electronic sound
                    mystical perversion
     the necessary assassination
     the assassin loving his victim
          cultish ritual
or clean admiration and direct response
                    Within the revolution
                              everything
          EVERYTHING!
     including imagination
                    discipline and organization
          confidence obviating need
                         for paranoid fantasies
          and competence in professional
               social and natural skills
I flow in and out of people's minds
          at stage one
     a metabolic system
                    talking
                      keeping silent
          taking notes
                    making friends
     endlessly frustrated
     yet content
that piercing the strangeness in anyone
          is exposing you

to me
in whom you have infinite trust

March 24, night

Niña Bonita
beautiful child
young F1 calves
and infant Holsteins
grazing in experimental pasture
or mooing expectantly
for their 8-quart diet
hoofs wading through shallow
blue concrete pool
secretly protecting them from fungus
mothers in air-conditioned barns
green clover-like food
in piles before them
water fountain two can share
We walk between two facing rows
patting damp dog-noses that sniff and shy away
then pass them in the rear
a girl bends down to tie her shoelace
and green grassy turds
flow luxuriantly through muscular opening
with nonchalance
"What did I do wrong?"
buses take us to plots of experimental pasture
then across road to mini-reservoir
where Henry tries to balance himself
on palm trunk
floating by pond plants and small fishes
and falls in with his pants on
Finally we go to newly constructed prefabricated homes

for farm workers
almost everything is free
a Cuban explains
as shutters creak with eerie freshness
we visit workers and childre
play in playground
look through homes
"This is better than the place *I* live in!"
elsewhere beer and sandwiches
under mango trees
near coffee plants
then travelling back to camp
past Miramar embassy mansions
filled with scholarship students
along Havana shore
sleeping
reading Whitman
talking
thinking about one woman or another
I met here
silence returning
the expressions on their faces
Niña Bonita
"You must remember
nothing like this
ever existed in Cuba
before the revolution"

nighttime

Inspiration
can it come from thinking of Native Americans
who spoke about themselves
this evening?

mentioning in passing
returned brigade members
helping out the Indians at Alcatraz
makes me think
how I'd want to stay with the brigade
somehow after returning to the States
meanwhile complaining
how interruptions constantly occur
when I try to get my head together here
"It's time for me to sack out"
but I give myself an hour
risk poor cutting tomorrow
to struggle the way I'm used to
under verbal barrage
from otherwise silent mouth
lately having trouble talking
while others talk privately or secretly
going somewhere with a problem
a collective responsibility
to be present when someone has troubles
so they won't spread like ink
into unproductive self-indulgence
another problem
not taking initiative
taking an interest in the way one's life is run
or routine organized

*

Some time ago
Eva and I started talking
after initial friendly joking
then we stopped talking
undergoing small periods
of personal frustration

unwilling to submit these feelings
to collective
we have experimental faith in
two days
"tired of collective living"
returning to the fold
somehow changed
unless my paranoia distorts
Dealing with problems
"Maybe I'm naive . . ."
"I know I'm inarticulate . . ."
But I'm very articulate
so I don't have strong reactions
setting myself loose in the wilderness
to meditate on and adopt
a frog's or a vulture's soul
returning to the collective
tribal life of
all life
all objects
"Can you tell if this is written
by a man or a woman?"
frustrated by my refined state of mind
unable to relinquish my will
to a teacher
or any longer to a process
or collective experience
I want my own room
my free evening
sick pay
I want a collective experience
all by myself
that I won't have to share
I know eight, ten . . .
fifty people in the camp

                    being with
        the smiles that blow my mind
                        which articulation spoils
                    afraid to be reduced to a line in a poem
            when you are a poem
                        pat on the back
                "I don't have to be told
                            how much everybody loves me"
                    instead of
            "Tell me that you love me
                        even if you don't mean it"
                        I love to hear your name
                F1
            total chaos
                    let things flow
    I should tell someone
            that I love a lot of people here
                and don't know what to do about it
                            it's a personal problem
        A morning off
                    in canefield dripping with dew
                        looking for small animals
                some threatened lizard
                            puffed-up frog
                        vultures in sky eternally
                or reading Walt Whitman
                            about the bodies that pass him
                                    he loves
                    must seek out and get to know
                or Eva's curiosity
                        as if she were the only earthling
            my poverty of collective skills
                    I've come here to struggle with
        along with the cane

March 26, afternoon

Wind is billowing up the tent
all windows open
light through nylon screens
relaxing the contrast
like a special movie filter
taking time out
because of long lunch line
a little more than one week left
of cane-cutting
last night a press conference
with international correspondents
We all attended
expecting controversy
which never showed up
plugging in our Japanese earphones
for simultaneous translation into English
of Spanish and Russian
I puffed on my cigar
couples plugged into same transistor
on benches in Recreation Hall
movie *Lucia* postponed because of tedious questioning
the day otherwise resplendent
beginning with volunteer work
at early hour of 6 AM
alone on the road for a change
to see earlier sun rising
hard morning chopping
nearly finishing the field
During *merienda* break
of cake and orange drink
Will describes previous night's meeting
to choose people to be questioned by press
Cuban delegation head's
reprimand

not to become obsessed with procedure
after two and a half hour meeting to choose three people
Then we elected Elsie
to attend another meeting
to choose someone to greet the North Koreans
who will be arriving this afternoon
After more morning cutting
middle top toss
bottom toss
screwed-up calculus of typical irrational growth
exceptions outnumbering rule
I returned to camp and took a shower and ate
talking with Mary
a Cuban working with us
who wanted to know what I'd be doing
back in the States
whether I agree with Weathermen
I said I'd have to talk to people
to see where I'd fit in
more questions
Vietnamese music like Brahms piano sonata

later

Fidel comes to look
at two different cane-cutting machines
the Rube Goldberg *Libertadora*
and the newer sturdier faster Henderson
he cuts cane with another brigade
a short distance away
but we don't see him
only hear of him
and see a piece of candy
he gave to someone
later on

We see from a great distance
          the machines doing what we're doing
     and stand amazed
Eva and some others
     freak out
          "Fee-DEL! Fee-DEL!"
     we get yogurt for *merienda*
               which means ice cream at night
a press conference too
     the man who collects and dumps our garbage passes by
               This cane!
               "Fuck!"
          fall down in frustration
               yells from the gut
     and the *merienda* comes at 5:15
                    an hour late
                    but we have fun
               suddenly quit early at 6 PM
     hop on *alzadoras*
          that pick up our cane piles
               for ride partway home
     waving hats and hands
          then final run to camp
               I shave for Fidel
               who's gone by then
     and take a shower
               eat with Will who describes
          press interview experience of his
                    opposing assumptions of interviewer
                    and interviewee
     Now got to eat
     I hope line's smaller

March 27, night

        Typing the love
                 down the recorder
     speaker
          su atención por favor
   I come the distance
       amphetamine
       deodorants
      here to Cuba
  dying to get the bright
      down here
          chromium
        cars autumn
        sumption
    along tracks
        directly passenger
           corresponding to the peanuts
in the genes
     together with tiny tree frogs
         almost machete-slashed
     this day by other brigade
       otro brigada
   in the fields
     distant and alone
questing for God
   the cause
   (in capital letters)
      the leaf has a function
    please come to the telephone booth
  writing from where I come from
starting to hop down
     like a frog
      named Johnny

     *

My throat burns
                from sweet orange drink
            lying down at *merienda*
yesterday North Koreans
            cut with us
        one pointed to his wire mesh goggles
                        implying I should play it safe too
            but I said
                "No hay"
            and that was that
        covered with
                    insect repellent
        driving him crazy
                    in the night
            malicious ripping down of mosquito netting
    crazed by bugs
                tractors picking up cane
                        two blue and bright red bugs
                fucking on one of my piles of cane
        la caña
    the canine
            Bon-Bon
    "Get out of the fucking bed, Bon-Bon!"
                        tiny black Cuban puppy
            taken in by lonely Americans
    just me free associating here
                in the Book Tent
            the noise
                the infected sore on my foot
    not mine
            Mark's
    accepting easily other personae
                I am all people
                    etc.

                    *

The Koreans worked well
                 first cutting and cleaning the cane
                 until told
                 "No caña limpia"
                 we cut "dirty" cane
            for the cane-conditioning center
                          the *centro de acopio*
                 which blows out the leaves
            and other useless or destructive light garbage
                          a gravity system
                 "Tell me all you know about ABM"
                 on the lunch line
                      a lecture
        then talk of dead Cuban bull
                 whose semen is still used
                          for artificial insemination
            Fidel's kindly attitude toward it
        the Koreans
                 los Coreanos
            ceased cleaning leaves from stalks
                      and speeded up
                 so Kevin and I
                      no longer could keep up
    at *merienda*
        we talked
            asked them questions about North Korea
                 their ages
                 one as young as 18
        their names
                      Kim
                 Chung
        Adelia finding out some Korean words
                      I smoked a Korean filter cigarette
                 though I never smoke
los Coreanos take second afternoon break
                 at 5:30

so we talked more
then cut more
taking their gloves out of their attaché cases
At 6:30 we left the field
and they distributed Korean books
magazines and postcards in color
"Kim Il Sung's Reply to . . ."
in gilt lettering
fields of Korean wheat

*

They're bigger
stockier
than the Vietnamese
had to get used to the warm weather
brought most of their own equipment
to the *zafra*
supplied by their own government
including machines to pick up cane
food and medicine
political commissars
machetes
the Third World self-reliance
we've heard so much about
high growth rate
they brought a film on their country
I didn't see
full of steel mills
and other machinery
They march to dinner
but kindly and smiling
those near us joking all the time
telling us to stop for the break
when we cut a minute longer

                              out of kindness
                    and respect for discipline
                         we're so unaccustomed to
          I stood aloof from them
                    not knowing the language
                              even much Spanish
                    smiling
          hope that gets across
                         walking mostly alone
               down the road
                    wondering if they think I'm the spy in their midst
          such typical paranoia
                              how can I take it seriously anymore?
          singing song about illustrious leader Kim Il Sung
                              phrase by phrase
                    on way home
                    sweetly
          and we nevertheless forget all the Korean words
               Kim in the presence of the workers
                              who write stories about their
                                   encounters with him
                    put into a book we look on
                    like early edition of the gospels
          illustrious lithographs
               patient a-priori reasoning
                         with dull-witted neutrals
                         and "progressive" student "elements"
          CO_2
                    H_2SO_4
                    Mendeleyev?
          I ask everybody around me
                              much uncertainty
                    John wanders by outside
               intoning our names like a ghost
Public Health Conference

going on in Rec Hall
I'm not attending
Oh yes
2000 dinners served two nights ago
to the 1000 people here
because there was ice cream
and many returned
for seconds and thirds
getting others angry
with an honest collective spirit
next night more ice cream
which is unusual
and the same thing happened
people sneaking around
in disguise second time around
Naive person
apologizes to Cubans in kitchen
running out of food
"That's all right.
We know who we're dealing with."

*

Elizabeth with problem
of how to stick up sign
announcing photo meeting tomorrow
so I run out to get Scotch tape

*

Still haven't announced tonight's purpose
Eva came into tent and left
to go for a walk
other person typing at this table
I feel as if I'm growing compulsive

                    like this metal cup
                don't drink anything hot in it!
            Is she a poet too?
    I want to meet them all
                somehow my mind's not operating
            this field is full of thumbnail size tree frogs
                I almost chop them up as I seek elusive cane roots
            Brigade 10 cut 10,000 *arrobas* today
                            a new record
                    so maybe Fidel will cut with them next week
            our last of cutting for the *zafra*
                    before our Caribbean island tour
                            of two weeks
            from Santiago de Cuba to the Isle of Pines

                                *

            Random information
                of an unpoetic nature
                    an irrelevant concept
                            we think in collective terms
                    an experiment of some sort
                            no North American collective can
                                be like this
                    discussing all the time who you can trust
                    so you can discard your responsibility
                            and blame procedure
                        or let it be automatically flawless
                                as a social dream
                    with no bad love affairs either

                                *

            A craving for grapefruit just passed over me
                live canned or just plain juice

pink or light yellow
I can taste it on my palate
my tongue
my stomach
my lips getting itchy from the citric acid
I'll buy one when I return to the States

*

In the last week or two
been pressuring myself
to come up with
neat thought packages
defining recent experience
so I might be forcing some things
and must watch out
still to live openly
judging only when necessary
not thinking except as useful response
tool not profession
profession of intellectual
tool for feeding family in style
making it
all movements of body thinking anyway
coming up with rationalistic snaky arguments
avoiding frightening reassurance of present time
and challenges
to jump into activity
anyway labeled evil
by Southern senators
be my body in it
the Dance
etc.
bullshit
etc. too

everything etcetera etcetera
I jump back into living
body movement bullshit mosquito bite scratching

March 28, night

A red light blinks from this perspective
across the fields
a knoll with caves I heard of
wish I had time just to visit
people mostly
a car caresses me with its fenders
it's late at night
we go to the beach tomorrow morning
which I look forward to
some Latinos
wanted to work on Sunday voluntarily
in solidarity with Latin American people
but camp direction decided no
no wind at night
I feel alone
though I'm so friendly
kind of throbbing
in a limousine of a body
lights from tent squares
blue control post party light
like subdued New York loft rumor
ping pong date
learn to respect sharp women
where's Eva?
I'm not thinking
few people pass by me
investigating cultural activity
lightweight

all itchy and damp from dirt and bugs
                              cigar taste in my mouth
          I'm alone tonight
          but don't feel so alone
      writing a poem about alienation
                        someone
                        a bright blue planet in the sky
              a hunger pang
      what's happening in the camp?
                  I want to wander around some more tonight

March 29, at the beach

    Just out of the water
            Arroyo Bermejo
        using unlockable locker 125
                            third straight time here
                wet hair on legs
            tiny bugs a smudge on page
    small black lamb tail wag
                like a shudder
                    near road in recess
        first appropriately bright hot sunny day
                    in three tries at beach
    a woman's meeting under coconut trees
                75 yards off
            near bus parking lot
                    me in usual prickly grassy area
        stop to look at frail efficient light blue fly
    sand on my feet
                reminding me of Whitman
                        clouds thin smears
                bicycle seat squeak
    I swam out to coral protrusion

and stood on seaweed 200 yards out
expecting more and more of myself
floated on my back toward shore
whistling and humming
listening to submarine sound
of my harsh voice and breathing
two small chattering black birds
in coconut palm that gives me shade

March 31, afternoon

It's breezy
and the pressure's mounting
possibly too much to take in
and expel
profound
a small puff
or presage of events
something leading from here
walking out of a tent
to the luxuriantly thick atmosphere of home
I crave now
as refuge as well as challenge

*

So tired
we get to know each other so quickly
that's what's been happening
along with a low level of consciousness
of what's going on
This is home
a home
made that way

partly by us
and we want to leave
only if we leave together
and stay with each other
at least have the feeling
we strike each other over distances
like bombs of feeling
in letters
or through what reminds us of each other
I guess now
I'm hardening myself
for disappointed partings
too many addresses to take
people lost elsewhere
not where I'm going
home to individualist battlefields
or other battlefields

later

Home to Eva
the spirit
of our brigade
I thought that's true
that she's the spirit
though she doesn't belong to us
or to anybody I know of
and might resent a thought like this
but I think about her so often
that thought was inevitable
like monkeys at typewriters
a silly obsession
a compulsive talker
learning to keep her mouth shut

                    her eyes from roving
            totally distracted
                        elsewhere
        down home to Eva
            watermelons
                    track
    travel
        Everyone's afraid she'll go off somewhere else
                especially the wan and quiet
                        middle class
        she finds here in abundance
    we all want her approval
                and suddenly fear shows up in her shaky voice
                a slight whine
                a quiet self-deprecatory remark
        the middle class can forgive itself
                    and love itself
            every day of the year
        instead of thoughts
                curiosity and astonishment
                close calls
            and scar tissue
    staring ahead blankly
            responding with words innately moving
                biting her lower lip

night

                I wandered around
            looking for Trude
                    to reassure myself
        I hadn't made a mistake
            showing her my journal
                    looked in her tent

                    the dining hall
                              film theater
                         Communist Party seminar
                              control post
            and Recreation Hall
                        now feel some apology is in order
                                        still afraid of accusations
                                                of male chauvinism
                    in my deepest blue mind
                    I'm depressed
            my cigar makes me dizzy
                                    the heat and dampness
                              and millions of mosquitoes
                        contribute to my mood
People shouldn't be at meetings or movies
                                    when I want to talk to them
                    There's so little time
                    and I don't believe in work
                                    under some circumstances
            when I'm trying to be honest with myself
                              work it off
                        in the canefield
                                    walk faster
            enjoy being soaked to the skin
                        make indirect gestures
                              to people
                        to signify my mood
            they see
                        but they aren't sure

                                    *

I feel very uncomfortable and annoyed

                                    *

Not the right time to talk
and feeling tense
like in the States
What am I doing typing
except acting compulsively?
It's tough to find someone
not busy
among the 700 here
but I have to look
Where's my celebrated
personal development?

April 3, afternoon

Friday
of our last week
finishing a field
in pale heat
from windless light blue haze
Koreans
Vietnamese
Africans
Latin Americans
and miscellaneous exiles
cutting with us
My partner is Will for the first time
so I have to push to keep up
and we complete nine piles in the morning
sweat pouring over my glasses
distorting vision
so I go into myself
hearing myself work
At *merienda* of warm cola and cake
lying all of us
on long flat cane leaf mattress

        I say
   déjeuner sur l'herbe
             and the world weaves
backwards
        to New York
               France last century

late night

                Record of an event
                      that happened the day after
                      the Venceremos Brigade
                completed cutting its third million
                         three million *arrobas* of cane
                      cut
                        placed in large one or two ton piles
                 made neat at end of morning
                         or end of afternoon
           in half hour specially laid aside
                  Today Will and I cut nine such piles
                              in the morning
           we finished the field of Cuban cane
                    in the afternoon
         with the rest of our brigade
                      fucking off sometimes
            to chase and get fear chills
                     from rats
                  cornered in last clump of cane
             or frogs
                  white nearly
           or dark or light green
      of different sizes
                     even the blue and red flying bugs
                      homeless

108

                    and no nearby field —
            all of them cut by Americans
with wild but polite slashes
            dedicated to work
                        or political symbolism
            but nevertheless
            accomplishment
                        for rich ones like us
The serious ones
            the ones aware of not being slaves in work
                singing
                    sleeping
                talking
            hiding under long cane leaf cover
                        refusing because tired
                to make piles neat
                or work at all
                        beyond a point
        It's good
                you know
        I just don't want to see another grain of sugar!
                    even to presume
            each stalk is a Yankee
                            whose head must go
                leafy brainless brute
                legs cut from under
                        previous stability obtained from lack of
                        historic challenge
                from peoples deprived of sunlight
            covered in dead leaves
        imagination rhetorical
                for a *norteamericano*
            suffer through plebeian insights

                        *

I'm staying up late
it's after midnight
and a half day left of cutting
our last in Cuba
probably our lives
no more agricultural labor of any type
five grains
salt tablets
broken handles on water jugs
tapes in this tent
of speech and interviews
peripheral to our work
mosquitoes I somehow tolerated this long
coming to scout my ankles and wrists
this insect repellent
Union Carbide's failure
we got home to tent camp
stood on line
hoping for special meal
getting *La Especial* cigar
with gold band
milder and shorter than usual
but still strings of meat
sweet potato
rice and beans
but brand new watercress or clover vegetable
slightly peppery
"Look at that girl over there
She was on the Bolivian border
trying to get in
when Che was killed
She and her boyfriend wandered all over Latin America
When she walks
she holds her back perfectly straight
You can just go over to her and say
'Tell me about South America!'"

                    an English girl
                            with a Texan husband
        a Cuban band in corner of dining hall
                                    Latin American exiles
                                            cutting with us
                    were told how dedicated we were
        then wondered at our slow pace
                        the Vietnamese
                            from North and South
                            with us for three days
        the Riders of Chullima brigade
                            of young North Koreans here too
                and Africans from the Congo and Guinea

                            *

At least two small rats
                        running through masses of cane leaves
        a white luminous frog
            jumping in brush
                        lost in specific leaves
                    visualized as mass
        in spite of familiarity of six weeks
                        with view of the field
        To see every mote in cloud
leaf on tree
                    instead of vague vain masses and movements
                Our next project
        leaving single stalk for each of us
                    as ideal canefield memorial
                        cleared of debris
                    abstractly delineating an acre
                we cut them simultaneously
                        each of us at the base of a stalk
        they go down
                    the ceremony

                    our game
        then back to final piling
                    cranky *alzadoras* move in
                        Strangely an oxcart full of cane
            walks heavily down road
                    like pre-revolutionary museum on wheels
                            more nostalgic than old Buicks
        songs
            including the Grand March from *Aida*
                    and "He'll Be Comin' Round the Mountain"
                referring to Fidel
    with improvised verses
                hoping he'll show up today
rum for *merienda?*
                        oranges and cake
        "There'll be rum for *merienda*
                        when he comes . . ."

                        *

        Will and I wait on hard bench
                    with hundreds of others
                our earphones and transistors between us
                        smoking cigars
            standing up
                    looking around
        sitting
                    getting tired of both
                        man with beard over there
            O my eyes!
        It's so easy to spread a rumor
                    just let someone overhear you use
                        words like "ice cream" or "Fidel"
        and people's ears burn
                    like canefields

prepared for Henderson mechanical cane cutter
one such field lit up sky tonight
like Bannet's comet falling in morning
over mill
past dining hall
channel 2 on transistor
static elsewhere
English translation of speeches
almost 10 PM meeting starts
a black sister reads speech from us
about our unity
in concrete act of solidarity
with Cuba and rest of Third World
and learning about the need for unity back home
Banner commemorating third million
presented to her
and Cuban gives speech
Then political song and three fireworks
we clap in time
and run around to Rec Hall
get on line
to receive rum and orange drink or cola
band finally strikes up dance sounds
and high talk
over outdoor party scene
field burning in distance
many greedy Americans
pursue seconds on rum
depriving others of firsts
like the ice cream incident a week ago
such impulses and assumptions and habits
retained as reminder
of strength of socialized behavior patterns

*

Adelia given *Mambises* soft straw hat
                                several of us try on
                        Ted grimaces at rum
                                and gives most to me
                which I share with others
                        my shortened cigar
                        quietly given in cigarette lighting ceremony
                to black woman at dance
        Richard with seconds in his stomach
                                gets drunk and sick
                        Vietnamese laughing in small bunch of others
                        everyone has his own button
        many with *trimillonaria* T-shirts we got last night
                                three large colorful
                        three-dimensional-looking stars
        Barbara pissed of at missing rum
                because of those who had seconds
                        several artists painting new commemorative mural
couples and individuals
                        a comet
                        like in *War and Peace*
        we really did cut tons of cane
                                and now we go on tour
        to Havana and the provinces
                        no finality to the experience
                        which I prefer to prolong
                the excess of pleasure
                                not severed from people
                the public anticipation
        of future acts and history
                        divulging fantasy secrets
                        a violent death
                rebellious youth
        a real political act
                        of international scope and significance

hard agricultural labor we pulled through
but if we don't enjoy it
how long can we postpone pleasure
for the sake of revolution?
how that postponement will embitter us!
a full life
for the revolution
not a mechanical role!
and the fear of wimping out
enough rum in a waxed cardboard cup
to expose softness
vulnerability
presence of body
alone and together
longing and touching
between work
and political actions
with goals
Organisez-vous!
"Do you trust me?" I ask
after Paul's conceptualization of trustworthiness
in the third person
"Someone who . . ."
wandering dinner line
precious sleep
and food
dried orange rind
with cigarettes and ashes
full life and discipline
"If I lie
it's for your own good"
everyone's asleep
but those in Book Committee tent
typing and listening to tapes
talking over bus charter arrangements

                    from Montreal
            to coasts mountains and plains
    I have a deep tan
            and hard cane cellulose bunk board waits
                    5 AM
                the comet again
    my Cuban adventures continue

April 4, afternoon

                    Peeking up through hole in trees
                to hole in giant clouds
        just had lunch
    two girls singing
                what sound like show tunes
                    no music from speakers
                        just occasional announcements
            a phonecall for someone
                        Cuban or American
    sleeping bags laid out on gravel
                    bodies laid out on them
                trees lightly rustle
                    you feel the day won't get more intense
        a peek at feedback
                small band and some dancing in dining hall
                cleaned up
                        no underwear
        talk with John
                Eddie comes by
                        Roberto and Renato
        Joe has his picture in *Bohemia*
    a meeting is called
                    of the whole brigade
            at the basketball court
        endless leisure

fucking off
we finished all six weeks of work this morning

[Began to write a poem, when a quick meeting was called (after lunch), announcing Fidel was here and we would cut with him in afternoon. We put on dirty clothes for the last time and went to new fields, burnt ones easy to cut, and cut most of the afternoon. Fidel was in separate brigade with one person from each of 25 brigades. Henry from ours. Returned, heard stories of Fidel from H. and others. Hung around volleyball court area until Fidel arrived at 8 or so. Buffet dinner (great!) served outdoors while F. talked in group up front. Then he answered questions for a couple of hours. Spoke beautifully. Got fine feeling from him. Got up close when he left. Eva shook his hands. Then a party: dancing, lots of rum. Everyone very stoned. To bed late, at one or later. Hard to believe no more cane cutting! Wow! The whole scene is "heavy" here and internationally.]

April 5, (to be continued)

Sitting around
Sunday morning
almost 9 AM
I have no hangover
from two big rum and colas
and party of release last night
wearing my *trimillonaria* T-shirt
talking to Kathy drunk
dancing in volleyball court
the strangest day in Cuba
and now quiet morning
waiting to board buses to Havana
after popping head
from warm mosquito net
into bright cool humid air

                    helping to put tables back in dining hall
                       two Vietnamese alone awake
                                looking towards fields
                           emptied of cane
               yesterday Fidel cut with us
                    in the afternoon
               when we were called back to fields
                           after illusory
                       final morning of work

later (unfinished)

                       Sunlight on page
                    waiting on palm-lined road
                           for other buses to catch up
                       the heat making me perspire

[Left on buses for Havana at 9:30. At Havana Libre had *merienda* in lux-
urious room in air-conditioned hotel. Then went not so far away to see
Robert and Meg with Trude, Judy, another Judy, and Lucy. Robert had
to go to work and I went there with him, met English woman and husband, saw Radio Havana offices. Ice cream nearby. Walked alone back to
see Meg. Girls eventually left. Tried to talk with her, but kids noisy,
though beautiful. Decided to stay late. Ate good home-cooked food —
potato salad, noodles, birthday cake, milk. Robert home at 6 or so. More
talk, though rushed. Gave them my typewriter, books, pens, etc. Caught
late bus (from brigade) at 8 PM, seen off by Robert and 3 older kids.
Mostly Cubans on bus. I stood most of the way. Back at 10 PM. Must
pack. Brushed teeth and talked with Eva, Wendy, Barbara B. Then with
Trude. Everyone loved Meg and Robert.]

April 6, afternoon, at sea on way to Isle of Pines

A big boat
high and fat
ferry from Batabanó
to the Isle of Youth
Elsie and Sandy joking
in fat green plastic-cushioned seats
large air-conditioned cabin
head rests
Elizabeth walks by
hair messy as a witch's
Sandy now reads
weekly English *Granma*
about Peruvian junta
and Bayamo cattle-raising
Elsie tries to sleep
Eva reading Marcuse's *Essay on Liberation*
Ted reading
looks blankly
twisting his fingers
out on deck
one to a spot on the rail
three decks
one with benches
my clothes feel uncomfortable
wearing loosely tied workshoes
hair in knots and scraggles
from sleep wind and sea
odd positions in chairs
sitting on arms
legs over arms

arms pushed to chair arms' rear for support
woman walks away
This morning
pins and keychains
with brigade insignia
tour program
map of Cuba
and decals
encouraging ten million ton harvest
four of them
then bus ride
down new road
through local Aguacate
and west then south
to Batabanó
to fill up ferry
with us and buses
three days' clothing
sleeping on black sands
in hammocks
with nylon covers
"like guerrillas"
"Bring your bathing suits!"
maybe we're out of sight of land already
a seven-hour ride
Eva and Sandy
lie down on floor
under back to back chairs
heads sticking into aisles
Elsie joins them
priorities
keychain irritates wrist as I write
hands smell of tamarind
sweet and tart
otherwise like dried apricots
Ted begins to sleep

someone suspiciously reading
The Divided Self
he must be thinking of schizophrenia
Ted moves to floor beneath seats too
Lots of sleeping
some soft talking or reading
For me
a walk and then some sleeping too

April 7, morning

I just awoke
a hammock
heavy clouds
the sea appearing close by
my chest cold under poncho blanket
bodies in long rows
all over
on beach of black sand
picnic tables
grass
a pig oinking nearby
roosters crowing
from different distant spots
walked with towel to large concrete beach house
for shit and shower
with other early risers
met Elizabeth outside
and found three dew-laden cigars
on the grass
short breakfast line forming already
photographers shooting hammock bodies
baby *plátanos*
Bibijagua
Isle of Pines

Bay of Batabanó
Cuba
camp area sprayed before our arrival
to remove mosquitoes
People with bad backs
worse from hammocks
smoky fire smell
my eyes round and heavy
nylon flapping
I'll try to dry out the cigars
and see everything

later

I touched a pig's nose
it jumped
we covered our hammocks with nylon
protecting clothes in it from possible rain
"Have you seen bus 4?"
"It was on its way to Alabama
last time I saw it."
Jamy throwing watermelon seeds at Eva
on bus
near José Martí's
exile home
"I'm gonna cut the rope on your hammock tonight
You better watch it!"
We got here
where kids work planting watermelons and limes
from our beach home for two nights
to visit talk and wander
Don't know what happens next
besides food
and I'm drifting off
too organized and stiff

from cane routine
with its luxuries
to give myself up to travel-learning
to bus chatter and sleep
questions and answers
revolutionary youth

April 8, 4 PM

Incredible looseness
rose noses
human hairy beings
fresh with blood inside
"Close the door please!"
or let the air-conditioning out
playing beautiful games
sunburn
on board Jibacoa
to Batabanó
through thin green reef
"Hey, what's happening?"
"We got a meeting tonight"
Books spread open
six hour calm sea ride
shallow bay
soft motor
the hum or light tenses eyes and forehead
bus horns
clever organization
Bonnie with straight back
Climbed steps to hilltop
this morning
to see half the Isle of Youth
reservoir with boats below us
orchards

many young pale rows
others lush shadowy bowls
of green rondure
a radio climbs my movie head
"The Blister that Beeped Its Way
Into the Heart of the Czechs"
A romance
flower print journey
my first tour
anywhere
through Cuba
to Bibijagua Beach
school for tractor-driving girls
orchard of watermelons
beneath marble mounts
cultivated by youths
getting two hours sleep nightly
two months a year
Peg's serious face
eyes blank
closed
arm in strange open position
on arm rest
brass departure music from pier
of Nueva Gerona
Cuban women with bras
American women without
depressed
so far by tour-tiredness
pace for seeing
and learning little
no talk with Cubans
eat lots of watermelon
grapefruit juice
beer

getting too ill to smoke cigars
cold in uncomfortable guerrilla-type hammock
with only poncho covering over clothes
nausea when I get on food lines
unable to fight bad health or tiredness
to make most of journey
plus my quiet observant nature
the discomfort
tiredness
and slight tension and touchiness
on the ferry
Roberto sleeps next to me
holding Mark's books on his lap
like coming home from beach
Lucy tries to piece things together
in her journal
Eva jokes and talks for others
a paroxysm of insight
or human contact
closeness
before it's too late
needed now
beep beep

April 10, night

Getting on bus
6:30 AM
Lucy's and Barbara's washed hair
black and red
drying side by side
as we ride to Playa Girón
beginning of ten day journey east

*

talk with Eva
when she comes from under
her gray blanket
friends at school
who project their own school
people who've liked my poetry
places we've been
I give her eye drops
for left eye irritation
it's hard to look into it
even when asked to see if it's bloodshot

*

The land crabs at Playa Girón
dark red
mostly dead from dehydration
or fatal highway accidents
the people in Zapata Swamp poor
a veteran speaks
we eat in sun
warm beer/salad/meat/potatoes
with fresh limes and guavas
while strange distant-sounding band
tapped and sang near blue-green pool
a dancer on concrete beam
of structure
then through the cooler photographic museum
for an hour
moved by martyrs' occupations
shoe worker
peasant
millworker
peasant

                              also in militia
                bus driver in militia
                                  civilian
          mounted black tank
                    still covered in nine-year-old American grease
                    B-26 engine
                              with one bent prop blade
          feeling hot and tired and overfed

April 11, 6:45 PM

                         I took a second shower
                in Santa Clara
                         this morning
                    after being tapped awake
                                        in lower bunk
                         by student
          "golden tobacco"
                    I avoided last night
                guava odor
          Will went right to sleep
                         speaking with Orlando
                              a student here
                    about hippies
                    and American film *Che*
          Mark speaking more French than Spanish to him
                    This morning
                    yawning after shower
          seeing Vietnamese students exercising
                              outside of dormitories
                now on bus having breakfast
          collecting mango juice in cans
                    from those
                    who don't like it

April 12, 10 PM

   Hot sun in buses waiting by sea
    icy dormitory shower in mountains

        *

 Meals
   buses
  sometimes both
    and tension in the heat
      of Camagüey
     with tiny biting ants
    fierce sexual aggressiveness
        warm finger clutch
      and bad smart-alecky joking
    feeling alien from new friends
    on bad bus trip
     each into his or her own
       journey of tiredness
        literature
     landscape
  head of beer and dormitories
   black music on portable phonograph
     numbered wooden canvas beds
   meeting Cuban athletes
     at workers' recreation center
  everyone acting without thinking
   brigades isolated in buses
 to be together again on ship home!
    or back in camp
   pee pee
     ka ka
    pipicaca
  in cane
    en masse

                    by the side of road
            too tired to inquire of culture
                            or even wave
            the collective falling apart
                        under weight of schedule
            and lack of work
                        plus failing health
            overfed
      I can't make the effort
                        I must go to sleep
      I'm in love
      no self-discipline in the heat

[Left Ciego de Avila at 4 PM and rode to Camagüey city, sleeping most
of the way. Will got letter from Selective Service, Adelia from her sister
with Conspiracy trial clippings from Feb., and N. from her husband announcing divorce proceedings. Very hot. Elizabeth came on strong to
me. Roberto challenged by Adelia and Lucy for machismo on bus.]

April 15

[To Cemetery of Martyrs with Martí's tomb and other heroes: Frank
País, Antonio Maceo, etc. Smelled of dead, very ornate cemetery. Back
to university for lunch. On buses again for Moncada Barracks, now 26
of Julio primary school. Got small performances from 4–5 preschool
and first-grade classes, recitations, songs, dances, somewhat regi-
mented, tho the kids were beautiful. Then out of town to Granja Si-
boney, tiny farm which was staging area for Moncada attack. Like at
Moncada, a photo exhibit with interesting stuff. Misty S. Maestra in
background. . . . Uncomfortable lately with Eva and Lucy. Others? . . .
Wandered around and listened to some good Afro-Cuban Oriente music. Feel lonely. No writing = No talking. Must File Tax on Return to
USA. Kim Il Sung's birthday! Apollo 13 astronauts in dire trouble! Big
anti-war demo in US cities.]

April 18

[Board the newer bus again and spent morning going to Holguín. Talked with Eva on the way and read more Whitman. . . . Lunch and talk with Ginny, Lucy's friend, about our revolutionary strategy. . . . Talked with Mark and read most of *Democratic Vistas* by the time we reached Camagüey after 6 PM. . . . Frances from Brigade 5 approached me about NY brigade poetry reading with Lucy when we return. Later she and I read poems with Andre and her husband as audience. Lucy showed up and we talked briefly. . . . Saw Eva again. Wendy, with her, mysteriously left when I showed up, making situation uncomfortable. Astronauts land safely!]

April 19

[Began long morning ride out of Camagüey. . . . Finished reading *Democratic Vistas*. . . . Tried to read *The Communist Manifesto*. Failed. More walking. Played with 6–8 goats in a field. Got real friendly with them. (Eva was watching me.) Then a nap in shade near pool. . . . Rizo announced invasion a day or two ago of about 35 *gusanos,* not many tracked down yet. Sabotage of sugar mills planned? What? Everyone serious. . . . Talk with Eva on bus about spies, paranoia, etc.]

April 21, 7 AM (dream)

Like a street in Washington, D.C.
A middle class Chinese family
leaves in a car
with screaming children
Coming from opposite side
of (up/down) staircase
another Chinese family
out for a walk
led by baby in carriage alone

                        screaming in tears
                   Gentle wise old father follows
              and we ask him if the baby was left behind
                          by other family
                          he says it's his
                      and he's out for a walk
                              to visit family that just left
                   Disappointed he leaves with his children
                     taking disappointment wisely

                                 *

                     Back in bus or plane
                       Eva's sitting with Jane

April 22

[Wandered out to fields last time, looked at ants, heard a bird. At 9 AM, a Brigade 6 meeting to choose delegate to help draft a VB press statement in Saint John. Eva nominated me, Will seconded it. I was chosen by acclamation. . . . When we got to Havana, *Luis Arcos Bergnes* not in dock, so all buses made two side tours around Havana, including through Revolution Square. Finally got to boat and boarded, saying goodbye to Renato and both Robertos. Waited out on deck for a while, then left Havana. Sea slightly rough. . . . Didn't eat much. Out on deck again. . . . Eva helping out wiping tables.]

HAVANA TO SAINT JOHN

April 23, back on Luis Arcos Bergnes

Totally
new orientation
grow cold
sleeping in shade on deck
sweat in sun on bow
find somewhere to evade cooking smells
flushed toilet smell
and fresh paint smell
Eva sits down by me for a while

(now)

April 26, afternoon

From behind
a girl reminds me of Michele
walking away down deck
I'm thinking of Eva
only one gull
out of dozens this morning
following the boat
76 degrees in New York
passing toward Cape Cod
to Saint John again
attending many meetings on board
many responsibilities
still people in brigade
remind me of friends back home
Mark like Mike

Francelle like Seyma
I'm here
        and there too
    my blue workshirt and blue sweater
                    over VB T-shirt faded orange
            Press Conference thought
        "Guess we'll have to have a meeting!"
        one of the few pleasures in life
    an excuse to see those we love

                        *

        My journal is full of blanks
        feeling dishonest with myself
                    if I write
                and repeat
    details of incomprehensible pageant of Cuban tour
                        sleeping on buses
                    eating and drinking
        together in red seats
                    that were
                        part of our experience
            I don't feel I need
        a fixed image
            of the recent past
    I want to see what happens next
            see my old friends again
            present my new friends to them
    and treat them equally with love
                    and a conscientious shove or joke
            sun on my back
                    my tanned hands
            nearly as aged as Eva's

April 27, afternoon

People fascinated by water
ballet exercises led by Lucy
Jamy for squat and thrust
Mary takes picture of our brigade
to take home to Cuba
a bunch of clowns
the last days
only anxiety about Customs
grabbing Cuban souvenirs
clothes books pins and posters
We're nearly in the Bay of Fundy
our resting place
the sea is delicate but racing
sun still high
above wide satin aisle
Lucy says I'm cynical about some things
I define it as pessimism or frustration
Kathy hasn't heard
my whole life story
Ecology meeting on bow
"What we should be discussing
is how ecology relates to the movement"
How far north we must be!
I don't feel as if I've been away
dealing with the same problems I dealt with then
with different people
who once they disperse
will begin to find
their former bond forced
camera shutters
shudders from the air
my eyes tense
nose stuffy

head hot
sea borne
still more people around
to rush and find

NOTES

In November of 1969, Native Americans of many tribes took over the abandoned government prison on the island of *Alcatraz* in San Francisco Bay.

The Conspiracy was another name for the Chicago Seven (Abbie Hoffman, Jerry Rubin, David Dellinger, Tom Hayden, Rennie Davis, John Froines, and Lee Weiner) who were tried for conspiring to incite a riot in Chicago during the 1968 Democratic Party convention. William Kunstler was a lawyer for some of the defendants.

"*History will absolve me*" is Fidel Castro's defense statement during his 1953 trial for leading an attack on the Moncada Barracks in Santiago de Cuba on July 26 of that year.

The Old Mole was a radical newspaper published in Cambridge, Massachusetts.

Los Siete de la Raza were young Latino activists who were accused of killing a plainclothes police officer in San Francisco.

Alzadoras pick up piles of cut cane from the field and dump them in vehicles that transport them to the mill.

An *arroba* is a measure of weight, approximately 25 pounds.

The *centro de acopio* is where cane is cleaned of leaves and debris prior to the milling process.

A *guagua* is a bus.

Gusanos are counter-revolutionaries.

Los Mambises were Cuban guerrilla fighters during the Ten Years' War (1868–1878) and the Independence War of 1895.

A *merienda* is a snack.

Pica-pica is supposedly a sort of thorny plant. I'm somehow skeptical of its existence. Cane leaves were troublesome enough.

De pie! means "On your feet!"

Populares and *Aromas Rubios* are cigarette (*cigarro*) brands.

Zafra means "harvest."